CANADIAN DIARIES AND AUTOBIOGRAPHIES

CANADIAN DIARIES
AND AUTOBIOGRAPHIES

COMPILED BY
WILLIAM MATTHEWS

UNIVERSITY OF CALIFORNIA PRESS
BERKELEY AND LOS ANGELES
1950

UNIVERSITY OF CALIFORNIA PRESS
BERKELEY AND LOS ANGELES
CALIFORNIA

CAMBRIDGE UNIVERSITY PRESS
LONDON, ENGLAND

COPYRIGHT, 1950, BY
THE REGENTS OF THE UNIVERSITY OF CALIFORNIA

PREFACE

This book is a companion piece to my <u>American Diaries</u> and <u>British Diaries</u>, and to a similar work on British autobiographies which I am now bringing toward completion.

The present bibliography lists both diaries and autobiographies relating to Canada; it covers both British and French Canada; and it includes both published and unpublished documents. It is presented as a non-selective guide to personal records relating to Canadian life.

It is believed that the bibliography will be welcomed, as my other bibliographies have been welcomed, as a tool for historical, antiquarian, and literary studies. The documents listed provide a generous representation of the patterns of life in Canada, as well as a panorama of Canadian history and Canadians of all ranks and occupations. The list should be of service to scholars seeking untapped sources about Canadian wars politics, economics, settlements, racial relations; about exploration, the fur-trade, farming, and industries; about social life, religion, literature, and the arts. It should prove useful for historians of districts and of individuals. Above all, it should be of interest to those who like to read about people, for included in it are self-portraits not only by the eminent and important but also by the obscure and insignificant; few of the latter will ever prompt the curiosity and energies of a biographer, but their own diaries and autobiographies are sometimes far better than any biography could be.

The documents are listed alphabetically, according to the writers' names. Apart from this, the list follows the pattern of my other bibliographies. Each entry gives brief biographical data on the writer, the time span, brief notes on content and sometimes on interest, and a bibliographical record. These evaluations are usually based on general interest, but occasionally on historical value. In noting content, special attention is paid to matters of historical, sociological, and literary interest. The index attempts to give a serviceable guide to the chief subjects and places dealt with in the documents.

The material for the book was gathered partly in the United States and England, while I was collecting for my British lists, and partly in Canada. In the years 1946 and 1947, I examined the collections of the University of California, Henry E. Huntington Library at San Marino, Harvard University Library, Library of Congress, Yale University Library, the British Museum Library, Cambridge University Library, Bodleian Library Royal Empire Society Library, and the London Library. In the summer of 1949, I and my wife made a tour of Canadian libraries and supplemented our material from the Canadian collections in Queen's University, Victoria College and the other libraries of the University of Toronto, the Public Archives and the Parliamentary Library in Ottawa, McGill University, Montreal Public Library, and the Collection Gagnon, Bibliotheque St. Sulpice, and Laval University. Miss Florence Murray made a thorough search through the rich Canadian collection of the Toronto Public Libraries, and was also able to check numerous last-minute additions to the list and to reject a large number of books whose titles gave a false promise.

Manuscripts were examined in the Canadian libraries named but many of the items listed were contributed by Canadian librarians in response to a plea that was sent to all the Canadian libraries. It is certain that the manuscripts listed here are only a small proportion of those that actually exist, but the generosity of the librarians, from coast to coast, permits the inclusion of several interesting documents that have never been listed before.

The limits I have placed on the list should be carefully noted. I have excluded French material prior to the French and Indian Wars, material relating to the old North-West and the Pacific North-West except where it is clearly of Canadian interest, the diaries and travel books of Americans visiting in Canada, the diaries of fur-traders who worked in what is now American territory, the journals of world explorers like Cook and Arctic explorers whose travels were only incidentally in Canada. The writings of travelers in Canada are included when in diary form, but general travel books are included only when they have a distinctly autobiographical character. I must admit that I have sometimes transgressed these principles of exclusion and also that the application of them is necessarily highly arbitrary and subjective; but the absence of many documents which may occur to the reader is likely to be explained by the principles upon which I have worked. In my <u>American Diaries</u> there are numerous items of Canadian interest written by Americans which are not repeated here.

Although it is believed that a reasonable effort has been made to approach completeness in the list, it would be absurd to claim actual completeness. Especially in manuscripts and in documents which have been published in journals and magazines the list is probably very deficient. But if it lacks true bibliographical perfection, it is hoped that it has the virtues ascribed to the not altogether perfect automobiles advertised by the Los Angeles dealers, that it will provide "good transportation."

My acknowledgment of indebtedness is due largely to those same people to whom I have been so often indebted before. To the many librarians, English, American, and Canadian, who never failed in courteous helpfulness, the Regents of the University of California, and the John Simon Guggenheim Memorial Foundation, who helped me financially during my work, to Miss Florence Murray who worked so nobly in Toronto, to my friend Lou Kaplan of the University of Wisconsin Library, who passed on all the Canadian items which cropped up in his collections of American autobiographies, and to Lois, who strengthened my efforts with her own enthusiasm and skill, I give once more my best if thrice-repeated thanks. Miss Macdonald and Mrs. Sobel did the excellent job of typing for offset.

WILLIAM MATTHEWS

Los Angeles, 1950

CANADIAN DIARIES AND AUTOBIOGRAPHIES

ABBOTT, Rev. Joseph (1789-1863, missionary). "The Emigrant to North America," Mercury (Quebec), 1842; republished in enlarged form as, Philip Musgrave (London, 1844). Adventures and experiences of himself and various other people; advice to emigrants. The second work presents the same material in fictional form. Although founded on Abbott's life, neither work is strictly autobiographical. 1

ABERDEEN AND TEMAIR, Ishbel Maria,Marchioness of (born 1856). The Musings of a Scottish Granny (London, 1936) in part relates to Canada. See also, "Recollections of Experiences in Canada," Temple Magazine, October 1899. 2

ADAMS, Joseph. Fifty Years' Angling (London, 1938). Including Canadian experiences. 3

ADAMS, Sophia, of Delaware, Ont. Private journal, April 1880-April, 1882;incidents of farming and domestic life near Delaware; precedes her father's diary in manuscript. MS, Toronto Public Libraries (typed copy). 4

ADAMS, Thomas (1831-1928). Private diary, June 1882-November 1900; incidents of farming work and life near Delaware,Ont. MS, Toronto Public Libraries, 4 vols. (typed copy). 5

AIKINS, Charles, of Sandwich, Ont. Travel journal, June-July, 1806. Ontario Hist. Soc. Papers and Recs. VI (1905),15-20. His notes on settlements and mills at Sandwich-York. 6

AINSLIE, Thomas. Military journal, June 1775-May 1776. Lit. Hist. Soc. Quebec Hist. Docs., 7th Ser. (1905) 11-89. Notes on the siege of Quebec by the collector of customs. 7

AKROYD, Charles H. (b.1848). A Veteran Sportsman's Diary (Inverness, 1926). Includes shooting and fishing, Canada. 8

ALBANI, Emma (1852-1930, singer). Forty Years of Song (London 1911). Includes her childhood in Canada. 9

ALBEE, Mrs.Ruth (Sutton) and ALBEE, William. Alaska Challenge (New York, 1940). Journey from Seattle through British Columbia, Yukon Territory, and Alaska, to Bering Strait; life there in the 1930's. 10

ALDERTON, Haddon. One Man's Meat (London, 1947). Ranching in Canada, 1913; his service during World War I in Philippines and France. 11

ALEXANDER, Sir James Edward (1803-1885). L'Acadie (London 1849) two vols. British officer in Upper and Lower Canada, Nova Scotia, and New Brunswick; seven years of military affairs, travels, natural history. Passages in the Life of a Soldier (London, 1857). Canadian experiences, 1848 to 1855; politics, travels, descriptions of towns and regions; Crimean War. See also, Transatlantic Sketches (London, 1833), two vols. Trips to North and South America, including Upper and Lower Canada, during 1831-1832. 12

ALEXANDER, Richard Henry. Travel diary, April-December, 1862; an overland journey from St. Paul's to Cariboo, B. C. MS, Provincial Library, Victoria, 246 pp. 13

ALLAN, A. A. ("Scotty"). Gold, Men, and Dogs (London, 1931). A Scotsman's life in the northwest from the eighties; travels and adventures with dogs; the Klondyke goldrush; life in Nome and Dawson; varied jobs. 14

ALLAN, Fletcher. Ports and Happy Havens (London, 1947). Theological student in the Canadian wilds; enthusiastic missionary work on prairie farms; then leaves pulpit. 15

ALLAN, George T. Travel diaries, March-July 1841, and November, 1841. Oregon Pioneer Assoc. Trans., 9th Annual Reunion 1881, 38-59. Records of a Hudson's Bay Company employee; at Vancouver-York factory with Ermatinger, and in Oregon. 16

ALLAN, William (died 1939). Memories of Blinkbonnie (Toronto, 1939). Religious experiences and musings. 17

AMERY, Rt.Hon. Leopold. Days of Fresh Air (London, 1939). Including climbing in Canada. 18

AMHERST, Jeffery Amherst, first Baron (1717-1797, commander). Journal of Jeffery Amherst, edited, J. C. Webster (Toronto, 1931). Military journal, 1758-1763; expedition to North America; attacks on Louisbourg; the Quebec, Niagara, and Lake Champlain campaigns; capitulation of Montreal. 19

AMHERST, Lieut. Gen. William (1732-1781, commander). Journal of William Amherst in America, ed. by J.C. Webster (London, 1927). Military journal, 1758-1760; siege of Louisbourg and military affairs up to the surrender of Montreal. The Recapture of St. John's, ed. J.C. Webster (1928). Military journal, 1762; notes on the recapture of St. John's. 20

AMOSS, H. E. Canadian Neighbours (Toronto, 1931). Travel and social life in Canada. 21

ANAHAREO. My Life with Grey Owl (London, 1940). Autobiography of an Indian girl; Indian social life and nature around Quebec; memories of Grey Owl, the Canadian author. 22

ANDERSON, Andrew, farmer. The Narrative of Gordon Sellar (Toronto, 1916), 90-129. Journal, June 1825-August 1846; daily notes on farming work in Ont., near Toronto; among Scottish emigrants. 23

ANDERSON, Right Reverend David (1814-1885, Bishop of Rupert's Land). Notes on the Flood at the Red River, 1852 (London, 1852). Day-by-day account of flood; rescue of Indians: abandonment of home; return. The Net in the Bay (London, 1854, 1873). Diary and autobiographical account of his missionary work and travel in the Canadian Northwest. 24

ANDERSON, James. Fur-trading journal, 1855-1858; exploration and trading from Fort Simpson, McKenzie River, to the mouth of the Great Fish River, via Great Slave Lake; work of the chief factor for the Hudson's Bay Company. MS., Provincial Library, Victoria, 141 pages. Also journal of an expedition to punish the murderers of Mr. and Mrs. Corrigal, Anderson Papers, ibid. 25

ANDERSON, Rev. John (b.1823). Reminiscences and Incidents (Toronto, 1910). A Scottish Presbyterian minister's work; experiences in Ottawa from 1839; congregations; religion. 26

ANDERSON, Thomas Gummersall (1779-1875). Travel diary, June-July, 1835. MS, Public Archives, Toronto, 19 pp. Superintendent of Indian affairs at Penetanguishene-Sault Sainte Marie; visits to Indians. 27

ANDERSON, W. K. Autobiography. MS, McMaster University, Hamilton, Ont., 19 pp. Life of a Baptist preacher in Canada in the nineteenth century. 28

ANON. Military journal, November 1745-November 1746; official diary of military affairs and news; translated from French.

E. B. O'Callaghan, <u>Docs. Rel. Col. Hist. State New York</u>, X (1858), 38-75. 29

ANON. Military journal, November 1746-September 1747; military events and news in Canada; an official diary translated from French. E. B. O'Callaghan, <u>Docs. Rel. Col. Hist. State of New York</u>, X (1858) 89-132. 30

ANON. Military journal, July-September 1755; march of French Army from Quebec to Lake Champlain; battle. E. B. O'Callaghan, <u>Docs. Rel. Col. Hist. State New York</u>, X (1858) 337-340 Penn. Archives, 2d Ser. VI, 334-338. 31

ANON. Military journal, October 1755-June 1756; military events and news in Canada. E. B. O'Callaghan, <u>Docs. Rel. Col. Hist. State New York</u>, X (1858) 401-406. 32

ANON. Military journal, April-November, 1756; British march, from Boston to Quebec; descriptions of Montreal and Quebec. <u>The Military History of Great Britain for 1756-1757</u> (London 1757), 26-50. 33

ANON. Military journal, August 1756; siege of Chouaguen (Fort Pepperell); translated from French. E. B. O'Callaghan, <u>Doc. Hist. State New York</u>, I (1850) 315-319. 34

ANON. Seminary journal, 1757-1759; kept by a director of the seminary of St. Sulpice, Montreal. <u>MS, Faillon collection, Ottawa Archives</u>. 35

ANON. Military journal, January 1757-September 1759; kept by an officer of the British 48th Regiment; Ticonderoga, Fort William Henry; siege of Louisbourg. <u>MS, Toronto Public Libraries</u>, 354 pp. 36

ANON. Military journal, 1758; defence of Louisbourg; military details; lively comments on French personalities. <u>Un Journal Inédit du Siège de Louisbourg</u>, edited Léon Jacob (Paris, 1913). 37

ANON. Military journal, June-July, 1758; daily account of the siege of Louisbourg. <u>An Authentic Account of the Reduction of Louisbourg</u> (London, 1758) 60 pp. 38

ANON. Military journal, 1759;"an accurate and authentic account of the siege of Quebec." <u>MS, Ottawa Archives</u>, Case I-3. 39

ANON. Military Journal, 1759; Wolfe's expedition up the St. Lawrence, until the surrender of Quebec; kept by a British sergeant-major. A Journal of the Expedition up the River St. Lawrence (Boston, 1759); Mag. Hist., Extra No. 24 (New York, 1913) 97-113. 40

ANON. Military Journal, 1759; Wolfe's expedition to Quebec. Lit. Hist. Soc. Quebec, Hist. Docs., 2d Ser., No. 6 (1868), 19 pp. (from New York Mercury, December 31, 1759). 41

ANON. Military Journal, 1759; Wolfe's expedition to Quebec; among the papers of his secretary. Lit. Hist. Soc. Quebec Hist. Docs., 4th Ser. No. 1 (1875) 21 pp. 42

ANON. Military Journal, May-August,1759; siege of Quebec; official French journal; translated. E. B. O'Callaghan, Docs. Rel. Col. Hist. State New York, X (1848), 993-1001. 43

ANON. Military diary, May-September, 1759; French account of the siege of Quebec. Quebec Archives Dept. Report (1920-21) 140-201. 44

ANON. Military Journal, May-September, 1759; narrative of the siege of Quebec; from viewpoint of a French non-combatant. Journal du Siege de Quebec, edited Aegidius Fauteux (Quebec, 1922). 45

ANON. Military journal, June-August, 1759; British account of operations at the siege of Quebec. Hist. Mag.IV (1860) 321-326. 46

ANON. Military Journal, June-September, 1759; siege of Quebec military and naval movements; bombardments. An Accurate and Authentic Journal of the Siege of Quebec (London, 1759); A. Doughty, The Siege of Quebec (1901) IV, 279-294. 47

ANON. Military journal, June-September, 1759; operations of Montcalm before Quebec; translated from French. E.B. O'Callaghan, Docs. Rel. Col.Hist. State New York, X (1858) 1016-1046. 48

ANON. Military journal, July, 1759; siege of Niagara; translated from French. Hist Mag., n.s. V (1869), 197-199 (from New York Mercury, August 20, 1759). 49

ANON. Public journal, 1775-1776; events in Canada. MS, Ottawa Archives; American Review X. 50

ANON. Military journal, November 1775-May 1776; chief events in the siege of Quebec; a lively account by a British garrison officer. Almon's Remembrancer (London, 1778), 1-34; William Smith, History of Canada (1815); New York Hist.Soc. Colls. (1880) 173-236.   51

ANON. Military journal, December 1775-May 1776; siege of Quebec; by a British artillery officer. Lit. Hist. Soc. Quebec Hist. Docs., 8th ser. (1906) 11-53.   52

ANON. Public diary, April-May, 1776; notes on the weather and general events during siege of Quebec. Lit. Hist. Soc. Quebec Trans. No. 22 (1898) 45-49.   53

ANON. Travel diary, May-September, 1776; from Hanover to Quebec via England; good narrative kept at sea by a Brunswick mercenary; translated. New York State Hist. Ass. Quarterly Journal VIII (1927) 323-351 (originally published at Frankfurt and Leipzig, 1776).   54

ANON. Sea journal, March-October 1792; a crew member's narrative of Vancouver's voyage to the northwest coast; Indians and country. Washington Hist. Quar. V (1914) and VI (1915) passim.   55

ANON. Fur-trading journal, 1799; kept at Rocky Mountain House Hudson's Bay Company. MS, Provincial Library, Alberta.   56

ANON. Travel journal, 1807; a French account of a voyage from England to Canada in Enterprise. MS, Ottawa Archives.   57

ANON. Prisoner's diary, November-December 1812; notes kept by American at Isle aux Noix; reflections on the evils of war. MS, Public Archives, Toronto, 7 pp.   58

ANON. Fur-trading journals, 1822-1823 and 1828-1829; kept at Fort Chipewyan. MS, Alberta Provincial Library.   59

ANON. Fur-trading journals, 1828-1830 and 1839-1842; kept at Dunvegan. MS, Provincial Archives, Alberta.   60

ANON. Travel journal, 1838-1841; contents unnoted. MS, Ottawa Archives.   61

ANON. Military diary, June 1838-June 1840; kept by a soldier of the 34th Regiment; march from Toronto to Windsor; events at Windsor. MS, Toronto Public Libraries, 17 pp.   62

ANON. Travel diary, March-May 1840; from Sussex to Liverpool; voyage to Prince Edward Island; social life and conditions there. MS, New York Public Library.   63

ANON. Diary, January, 1841; work among Indians at Sault Ste. Marie. MS, Public Archives, Toronto.   64

ANON. Travel journal, May-August, 1847; a voyage to Quebec in an Irish emigrant vessel; quarantine; ship pestilence. The Ocean Plague (Boston, 1848).   65

ANON. Travel diary, August, 1847; from Collingwood, Ontario, to Fort William, Lakes Huron and Superior. MS, Public archives, Toronto, 52 pp.   66

ANON. Travel journal, April-May, 1852; Liverpool to New York, Toronto, Guelph, Hamilton, Niagara, Kingston, and Montreal; notes on lands, roads, farming, houses. MS, Toronto Public Libraries, 29 pp.   67

ANON. (Morgan?). Fur-trading journal, September 1853-February 1858; kept at Woody Mountain; work of store, trading, trapping, MS, Mair Papers, Queen's University, Kingston.   68

ANON. Fur-trading journal, 1854-1856; kept at Fort Edmonton, Hudson's Bay Company. MS, Provincial Library, Alberta.   69

ANON. Fur-trading journal, September 1857-April 1858; kept at Fort Qu'Appelle Lake post, Hudson's Bay Company. MS, University of Saskatchewan.   70

ANON. Fur-trading journal, December 1857-December 1858; kept at Fort Pelly, Hudson's Bay Company. MS, University of Saskatchewan.   71

ANON. Military journal, October-November, 1871; kept by private soldier during the Red River rebellion. From Toronto to Fort Garry (Hamilton, n.d.).   72

ANON. Settler's diary; kept at Lloydminster, Sask., by one of the original Barr colonists. MS, St. Andrew's College, Saskatoon.   73

ANON. Settlers' narratives, 1890-1914; written by eighty-four settlers in Saskatchewan communities; the typed copy of entries in two contests sponsored by the Regina Canadian Club. MS, University of Saskatchewan.   74

ANON. "Experiences of a City Clerk in Canada," Leisure Hour, August-October, 1904. A Londoner's unfortunate experiences in the Barr settlement in Saskatoon in 1903; an unpleasant picture of misfortunes and miseries of pioneer life. 75

ANON. Park diaries,1917-1919; kept by rangers at Quetico Park Ontario. MS, Public Archives, Toronto. 76

ANON. "An Englishman in Western Canada," National Rev., XCIII (1929) 280-301. An ex-officer's experiences in Manitoba and the Canadian Northwest after World War I. 77

ANON. (R. Mytton?). Diary, 1930; relative to his opening of a pulp mill; but mostly reminiscences of Wakefield settlement during 1868-1879. MS, Ottawa Archives. 78

ARMSTRONG, Nevill A.D. Yukon Yesterdays (London, 1936). Thirty years in the Klondike; goldrush, hunting, mining, exploring; wild life of Dawson in the nineties. 79

ASHE, Lieut. Edward David, of Quebec. Scientific Journal, July-September, 1860. Lit. Hist. Society Quebec Trans.,(1861, 1927) 1-16. Journey from New York to Labrador; observation of eclipse of the sun. 80

ASHWELL, Lena (b. 1871). Myself a Player (London, 1936). Includes an account of her childhood in Canada. 81

ASKIN, Charles (born 1780, soldier). Military journal, July-September, 1812. Canadian Archives Pubs. No. 7 (1912) 235-248; Mississippi Valley Hist. Review I (1914-1915) 561-565. Services with Canadian militia; surrender of Detroit; Fort Dearborn massacre. Military journal, December 1837 and February-June, 1838. MS, Ottawa Archives. Military operations on the Detroit River frontier during the rebellion. 82

ASKIN, John (1765?-1820). Fur-trader's diary, May 1805-August 1810. MS, Public Archives, Toronto, 3 vols. Trader and superintendent at Amherstberg; personal, business, and weather notes. 83

ATKINS, T. Reminiscences of Twelve Years' Residence (Malvern, 1869). Includes travel in Canada. 84

AUSTEN, Kate. Northern Nurse: by Elliott Merrick (N.Y.,1942). Narrative of author's wife, told in first person;Australian girl's work as nurse in mission hospital in Labrador. 85

AUZIAS-TURENNE, Raymond (born 1861). Voyage au Pays des Mines d'Or, Le Klondike (Paris, 1899). Travel journal, January-September, 1898; to the gold mines of the Klondike. 86

AYLMER, L. A. "Recollections of Canada," Rapport de l"Archiviste..de Québec (Quebec, 1935). Narrative of his experiences in Quebec during 1831-1832. 87

B., J. C., French soldier. Travels in New France (Harrisburg, Pa., 1941). His experiences as soldier in French and Indian War, 1751-1761; life and events in the wilderness; Quebec; Pennsylvania; very personal and interesting;translated from French. 88

BÂBY, William Lewis. Souvenirs of the Past (Windsor,Ont.1896). Seventy years in Western Ontario; early settlements; general conditions; travel; amusing anecdotes. 89

BACK, Sir George (1796-1878, explorer). Narrative of the Arctic Land Expedition (London, 1836). An exploration journal, 1833-1835; expedition to the mouth of Great Fish River and to shores of Arctic; topography; Eskimo; Indians. 90

BADEAUX, Jean Baptiste (1741?-1796). War journal, 1775-1776. See, H. A. Verreau (editor), Invasion du Canada (Montreal, 1870) 163-220; Quebec Lit. Hist. Soc., Hist. Doc., 3d Ser., 1872-1873. French account of the American invasion of Canada. 91

BADEN-POWELL, Robert Stephenson Smyth, Lord. Adventures and Accidents (London, 1934). Including his military service in Canada. 92

BAILEY, Jacob (1731-1808). Frontier Missionary (Boston,1853). Selections from the diaries and papers of missionary, first in Maine, then United Empire Loyalist in Nova Scotia. 93

BAILEY, Joseph Whitman (b. 1865). Autobiographical documents. MSS,5 and 118, Bailey Collec., University of New Brunswick, 55 pp. (1) Childhood at the college, where his father was a professor; (2) Journey to Germany, France, and England, in 1914; (3) Journey to England and France in 1926. 94

BAILEY, Mrs. Laurestine (d'Avray) (born 1841). Reminiscences. MS, Bailey Collec., University of New Brunswick, 40 pp. Her childhood in Mauritius;later life in England and at Fredericton, New Brunswick. 95

BAILEY, Loring Woart (1839-1925, of Fredericton). Reminiscences. MS, Bailey Collec. in University of New Brunswick, 44 pp.(1) His recollections of Harvard; student life, studies, famous teachers in the fifties;(2) His recollections of the University of New Brunswick, 1861-1915; geological work and travel. 96

BAILLARGEON, Pierre. Hasard et Moi (Montreal, 1944). Contents unknown. 97

BAILLIE-GROHMAN, William Adolph (1851-1921). Fifteen Years' Sport and Life (London, 1900). Fishing, bearhunting, etc., in western U.S.A. and British Columbia. 98

BAINES, Henry Edward (1840-1866, soldier). The Cruise of the Breeze, (reprinted from Hunt's Yachting Magazine, 1863). A humorous account of a cruise on Lake Ontario in diary form; August, 1863. 99

BAIRD, Lieut. Colonel William T., of Woodstock, N.B. Seventy Years of New Brunswick Life (St. John, 1890). Education in New Brunswick; military life and service in Cana. ; Indian troubles and revolts; family affairs, life of settlers. 100

BAKER, Philip. The Wild Life of Revolution (Regina, 1936). An autobiography of childhood experiences in Russia; emigrated to Canada after the revolution. 101

BALDWIN, Harold. Holding the Line (Chicago, 1914). Personal narrative of service in 1st World War with 1st Canadian Division; Ypres, Yser, etc. 102

BALDWIN, Harold. A Farm for Two Pounds (London, 1935). Farming on Canadian prairie in Saskatchewan; before 1st World War; rough experiences and hardship in towns; and his success on farms. 103

BALLANTYNE, Robert Michael (1825-1894). Hudson's Bay (London, 1848). Six years' residence in territory of the Hudson's Bay Company; everyday life in the wilds. 104

BANWELL, Selwyn. A Frontier Judge (Toronto, 1938). Account of British justice in the earliest days of the Far West. 105

BAPTY, H.(1848-1933). Military diary, April-July 1885; adventures in the North West Rebellion of 1885; by a soldier in the 7th Fusiliers, London, Ont. MS, Toronto Public Library, 30 pp. (typed copy). 106

BARKER, Bertram. North of '53 (London, 1934). Experiences as a trapper and miner in the Canadian Far North, after the 1st World War. 107

BARKER, Lewellys Franklin (1867-1943). Time and the Physician (New York, 1942). American doctor's autobiography; section on his boyhood and education in Canada. 108

BARKLEY, Francis. Private diary, 1836; contents unknown. MS, Provincial Library, Victoria; also his journal for August, 16, 1792, ibid. 109

BARNEBY, William Henry (b. 1843). Life and Labour in the Far West (London, 1884). His life and travel in British Columbia, Manitoba, and Northwest Territory. 110

BARNES, Joshua N. (born 1830). Lights and Shadows of Eighty Years (St. John, 1911). Autobiography of a Baptist minister in New Brunswick. 111

BARNES, Capt. William Morris. Rolling Home (London, 1931). An autobiography of a Newfoundland seaman, 1864-1920; boisterous account of adventures and dangers under sail and steam; service with mine-trawlers in World War I. 112

BARTLETT, Captain Robert (born 1875). The Log of Bob Bartlett (London, 1928). His forty years' seafaring; family life in Newfoundland; sealing, codfishing, Arctic exploration with Peary, travel in Europe. 113

BARTLETT, Robert Abram (1875-1946). The Log of Bob Bartlett (New York, 1928). Autobiography of forty years of seafaring and Arctic exploration. Same as last book. 114

BARTON, Freddie. We'll Go No More A-Roving (London, 1937). A life of travels and adventure; in second half deals with his emigration to British Columbia, surveying of virgin forests, service with Canadian cavalry in France during World War I, and later with a draft board; and his labors in the service of contract bridge. 115

BATES, J.I. Scrapbook. MS, McMaster University, Hamilton, Ont. 110 pp. Autobiographical jottings of a Baptist principal in Canada, 1864-1878. 116

BATES, Roger. "Testimonial," Ontario Hist. Society Papers, VII (1906) 146-153. Reminiscences of early British settlements and pioneer life in Ontario. 117

BATES, Walter (1760-1842). Kingston and the Loyalists of the "Spring Fleet" of A.D. 1783 (St. John, 1889). Reminiscences of his part in the American Revolution, and emigration as a loyalist to Nova Scotia. 118

BAXTER, Arthur Beverley. Strange Street (London, 1935).Begins withboyhood and education in Canada. 119

BAYFIELD, Henry Wolsey (1795-1885, admiral). Surveying journals, 1829-1853. Lit. Hist. Soc. Quebec Trans. No.28 (1910) 27-95. Inspecting coasts and harbors around the St.Lawrence River. 120

BEALBY, John Thomas (b. 1858). Fruit-Ranching in British Columbia (London, 1909). Daily experiences of a British emigrant fruit farmer. 121

BEATTY, Reginald, of Melfort, Sask. Reminiscences. MS, University of Saskatchewan, 16 articles. The life of a Hudson's Bay Company clerk, 1874-1896; pioneer life and events. 122

BEAUDOIN, Jean (1662?-1698, missionary). Les Normands au Canada (Evreux, France, 1900). Journal, June 1696-May 1697; of an expedition made with d'Iberville from France into Acadia and Newfoundland. 123

BEAVAN, Mrs. F. Sketches and Tales (London 1845). Reminiscences of experience during seven years about the backwoods of New Brunswick, 1820's and 1830's; settlers' customs and manners. 124

BEGG, Alexander (1840-1898). Travel diary,1869-1870. MS, Public Archives, Ottawa. Including an account of the Red River expedition. Seventeen Years in the Canadian Northwest (London,1884; reprinted from Royal Colonial Institute XV, 1883-1884, pp. 181-220). Experiences in the Winnipeg district, 1867-1884; history of the West. 125

BEIQUE, Madame F. L. (b. 1852, of St. Hyacinthe, Q.). Quatre-vingts Ans de Souvenirs (Montreal, 1939). Her childhood and marriage, family life; public and political events; personalities. 126

BELAND, Henri. Mille et Un Jours en Prison a Berlin (Beauceville, 1919). His experiences in France during World War I; capture; German prison camp; French-Canadian doctor. 127

BELANGER, Fortunat (b. 1866). Mémoires d'un Cultivateur(Quebec, 1936). Farming in Montmagny; working with Agricultural Society; science, soil, religion; ventures in goldmining in Yukon. 128

[BELL, Edward ?]. Exploration journal, 1791-1794; kept aboard the armed tender "Chatham" during Vancouver's voyage in the "Discovery." MS, Provincial Library, Victoria (typewritten copy). 129

BELL, James Mackintosh (1877-1934, a Canadian geologist). Far Places (Toronto, 1931). His travels in Northern Canada, New Caledonia, Kirghiz Steppes, Jamaica, and Albania. 130

BELL, William (1780-1857, of Perth). Clergyman's diary, 1817, 1823-1853, and autobiography from 1780; Scotland into Upper Canada; life and work as Presbyterian minister at Perth. MS Queen's University, Kingston, 16 vols. A life of Bell, based on these journals and with long extracts is: Isabel Skelton, A Man Austere (Toronto, 1947). 131

BELL-IRVINE. Travel diary, 1870; account of Red River expedition. MS, Public Archives, Ottawa. 132

BELLOT, Joseph René (1826-1853). Journal, May 1851-September 1852; in search of Sir John Franklin. Journal d'un Voyage aux Mers Polaires (Paris, 1854). 133

BENSON, Samuel M. (1801-1876). Travel diary, June-August 1816; round trip from York via New York and Queenston. MS, Public Archives, Toronto, 16 pp. 134

BENSON, Wilson. Life and Adventures (Toronto, 1876). Autobiography of life in Ireland; emigration to Canada and pioneer experiences in Ontario. 135

BERNIER, Joseph Elzéar (1852-1934). Master Mariner (Ottawa, 1939). Autobiography of sixty years at sea, edited from his logs and yarns; Arctic exploration and adventures. 136

BETHUNE, Right Rev. Alexander Neil (1800-1879). Clergyman's diary, November, 1847; visits to Anglican churches in Upper Canada. MS, Public Archives, Toronto, 116 pp. 137

BEURLING, George F., and ROBERTS, Leslie. Malta Spitfire (Toronto, 1943). Canadian flyer's early interests in aviation; experiences in World War II in Europe; battle of Malta. 138

BIGSBY, John Jeremiah (1792-1881). The Shoe and Canoe (London

1850) 2 vols. Travels and personal experiences in Upper and
Lower Canada, 1818-1827. 139

BILKEY, Paul Ernest (born 1878). Persons, Papers, and Things
(Toronto, 1940). Casual recollections of a journalist who
entered newspaper work in Toronto in 1896. 140

BINNIE-CLARK, Georgina. Wheat and Woman (Toronto, 1914). Englishwoman's adventures on the prairies; purchase of a farm;
farming experiences. 141

BIRDSALL, Samuel (born 1785?). Recollections written in 1862;
childhood in Pennsylvania; after 1804, his life in Niagara
Peninsula, Upper Canada. MS, Toronto Public Libraries, 44
pp. (typewritten copy). 142

BISHOP, Hon. Charles. Years Around Parliament. A series of articles in the Ottawa Citizen, beginning September 15, 1945.
Political reminiscences in Ottawa. 143

BISHOP, Major William Avery (born 1894). Winged Warfare (New
York, 1918). His services with air-forces in France during
World War I; Canadian's air battles; his adventures and his
exploits. 144

BISSETT, James, of Lachine, Quebec. Journal, 1854-1855, 1858-1859; 1867; journey to Red River settlement; later to Hawaii; trading there. MS, McGill University, 6th Floor D 22.
Originals lent by Miss Bissett. 145

BLACK, Mrs. George (Munger) (b. 1866). My Seventy Years (London, 1938). Social and political affairs in the Yukon; the
gold-rush; Canadian M.P.; life in Ottawa and London. 146

BLACKJACK, Ada. Arctic diary, March-August, 1923; with Stefansson's Arctic expedition;domestic work at Wrangel Island.
MS, American Geographical Society Library;typed copy at the
University of Toronto Library. 147

BLACKSTOCK, Rev. W. S., of Toronto. Methodist's diary, 1854-1899; occasional notes of his ministry at Goderich, Clinton
and Toronto; introspection; reading; entertainment; prices.
MS, Victoria College, Toronto, Archives Dept., Pam. R. 138,
4 vols. 148

BLACKWOOD, Algernon. Episodes before Thirty (London, 1923).
Journalism in Toronto and New York; his personal and social
life. 149

BLAKE, Mrs. Catherine, of Montreal. Private diary, April 1849; short record of riots, occasioned by Lord Elgin's assent to the Rebellion Losses Bill. Canadian Hist. Review XV (1934) 283-288. 150

BODDY, A. A. By Ocean, Prairie, and Peak (London, 1896). An Emigrant Clergyman in British Columbia; his travels to Manitoba. 151

BOLDUC, Mgr. J. B. Zacharie. Lettres et Journal (Quebec 1843; 1845). Record of his mission in Colombia. 152

BOMPAS, Charlotte Selina (Cox) (1830-1917). A Heroine of the North, ed. S. A. Archer, contains her journal of missionary work in Northwest Canada; wife of the first Bishop of Selkirk, Yukon. 153

BOND, J. Harman. Military journal, July 1860; with Royal Canadian Rifles; Kingston-Fort Garry; movements, people, and places. North Dakota Hist. Quar. VI (1932) 231-238. 154

BONE, Peter Turner (1859-1947?). When the Steel Went Through (Toronto, 1947), Autobiography of a Scottish-born pioneer railway engineer; and the building of the Canadian Pacific Railway. 155

BOOTH, Lieut. William (d. 1827?). Military travel diary, July August, 1785; a lively description of men and places in the maritime provinces of Canada; kept by an engineer. Report Public Archives of Nova Scotia (Halifax, 1934) 42-51. 156

BORDEN, Sir Robert Laird (1854-1937). Memoirs (London, 1938) 2 volumes. His boyhood in Nova Scotia; law practice; public life and politics from 1896; premiership during World War I; imperial relations and Canadian parliament; his private and social life. 157

BORRON, E.B. Exploration journal, June-September 1883; travels and observations in Hudson's Bay area. Report on that Part of the Basin of Hudson's Bay Belonging to the Province of Ontario (Toronto, 1884). 158

BOSWORTH, N. Diary: records of a Baptist minister in Canada; Nineteenth Century. MS, McMaster University, Hamilton, Ont. 272 pp. 159

BOUCHER, Georges Alphonse (b. 1865). Je Me Souviens (Montreal, 1939). Not seen. Since found to be poems. 160

BOUCHER DE BOUCHERVILLE, R. T. V. War Journal, 1812-1814; a Frenchman's account of travels into Upper Canada; notes of war with the Americans. <u>Canadian Antiq. Journal</u> III (1900), pp. 1-168. 161

BOUCHETTE, Robert Shore Milne (1805-1840, of Quebec). <u>Mémoires</u> (Montreal, 1936). Family life in Quebec; publication of geographical works; his part in the 1837 rebellion; his imprisonment in Bermuda. Includes diary. 162

BOUGAINVILLE. Military journal, 1755-1760; military movements during the French and Indian war in Canada. <u>MS</u>, <u>University of California</u> at Berkeley; transcript in Public Archives at Ottawa. 163

BOULTBEE, Rosamond, of Toronto. <u>Pilgrimages and Personalities</u> (London, 1924). Canadian public affairs and public figures; World War I; travels, adventures, and work of a journalist and European correspondent. 164

BOULTON, Alexander Claude Forster (<u>b</u>. 1862). <u>Adventures, Travels and Politics</u> (London, 1939). Autobiography of his life in Western Canada, and later as Member of Parliament in England. 165

BOULTON, Major Charles Arkell (<u>b</u>. 1841). <u>Reminiscences of the North-West Rebellions</u> (Toronto, 1886). Military life with scouts in the Red River rebellion of 1869, and the Riel rebellion of 1885; impersonal military notes; social and political life. 166

BOURGET, Mgr. Religious journal, 1846; his second voyage into Europe. <u>MS</u>, <u>Ottawa Archives</u>; Archevêché de Montréal, Carton 9, Part 2. 167

BOURGET, Clermont (born 1884). <u>Douze Ans chez les Sauvages au Grand Lac des Esclaves</u> (Montreal, 1938). Experiences as an Indian agent and doctor, 1923-1925 in Great Slave Lake District. 168

BOWER, Fred (<u>b</u>. 1871). <u>Rolling Stonemason</u> (London, 1936). Includes travel and work in Canada. 169

BRADLEY, Arthur Granville (1850-1943). <u>Other Days</u> (London, 1912). Including a section of reminiscences of his life in Canada in the seventies. 170

BRADLEY, Mrs. Mary (<u>b</u>. 1771). <u>A Narrative of the Life of Mrs.</u>

Mary Bradley (Boston, 1849). A Presbyterian's personal and religious life; Christian experiences, temptations, prayer, life in St. John, N.B.   171

BRASSEY, Annie (Allnutt), Baroness (1839-1887). Travel diary, August-November, 1872; from England through Canada to Niagara, down Atlantic coast, and return. A Cruise in the "Eothen." (London, 1873).   172

BREYNAT, Mgr. Gabriel (born 1867). Cinquante Ans au Pays des Neiges (Montreal, 1945-1947) 3 vols. Early life in France; missionary work in the Arctic;first vicar of the Mackenzie; administration, travels, adventures, Indians, Eskimos; missionary and hospital work.   173

BRIDGE, Samuel. Travel journal, April 1806-January 1811; England to Quebec; living in Quebec and Montreal; work in West Indian trade; the business conditions; Canadian customs and character; Catholic life, religion, customs;very interesting. MS, Public Archives, Ottawa, 3 vols.   174

BRITNELL, John (1849-1927). Books and Book-Selling (Toronto 1923). Autobiography of sixty years of bookselling; a lecture given in Toronto.   175

BRITTAIN, Sir Harry. Pilgrims and Pioneers (London, 1946). It includes his travels in Canada; cultivating imperial relations.   176

BROWN, Audrey Alexandra (born 1904). The Log of a Lame Duck (New York, 1939). The lively diary of the life of a cripple in a hospital in British Columbia; details of patients; her philosophy in sickness.   177

BROWN, Jack. Under the Surface of Crime (Gardenvale, Q.,1934) A policeman's autobiography of ten years in England and Canada; case histories of criminals; comments on police systems and courts.   178

BROWN, Rev. R. C. Lundin, of Lyneal, Salop. Klatsassan (London, 1873). His experiences of missionary life, travel, and religion among Indians in British Columbia, in the sixties; hardships and perils.   179

BROWN, Thomas Storrow (b. 1803, of St. Andrew's, N.B.). 1837: My Connection with It (Quebec, 1898).Political reminiscences; journalistic and political work supporting revolutionary activities of Sons of Liberty; his exile.   180

BROWN, William. America (London, 1849). Including details of his residence in Canada and work as a tavern-keeper. 181

BRYDONE, James Marr. Narrative of a Voyage (London, 1834). A naval surgeon's account of journey with emigrants from Sussex in 1834, in diary form; via Ottawa River to Toronto and Hamilton; settlement at Blandford; topography. 182

BUCHAN, Colonel. "With the Infantry in South Africa," Trans. Canadian Military Inst., No. 11 (1903). Life with Canadian soldiers in the Boer War. 183

BUCHAN, Anna. Unforgettable, Unforgotten (London, 1945). Includes section on her life in Canada with her husband, Lord Tweedsmuir, Governor-General of Canada. 184

BUCHAN, John, 1st Baron Tweedsmuir (1875-1940). Memory Hold-the-Door (London, 1940). The autobiography of the Scottish historian and novelist. His life and work as Governor-General of Canada, 1935-1940. Also published under the title, Pilgrim's Way (Boston, 1940). 185

BUCKLEY, Rev. M. B. Diary of a Tour in America (Dublin, 1889). An Irish missionary-priest in Canada in 1870-1871; Canadian cities and customs. 186

BUFFALO CHILD LONG LANCE (d.1932). Long Lance (New York,1929) Autobiography of a Blackfoot chief. Customs of the Indians of Montana and the Alberta areas. 187

BUIES, Arthur (1840-1901). I, Reminiscences; II, Les Jeunes Barbares (Quebec, 1892).Literary reminiscences of a French Canadian journalist and author. 188

BULGER, Captain Andrew H.(1789-1858, Royal Newfoundland Fencible Regiment). An Autobiographical Sketch (Bangalore, India, 1865). Services in the War of 1812, at Niagara and in Michilimackinac area; army career, mainly 1812-1820. 189

BULKLEY, Colonel Charles S. Journal, 1865-1867; with U.S.Army Telegraph expedition, building lines through British Columbia to Alaska. MS, Alberta Provincial Library. 190

BULLOCK-WEBSTER, Harry (b. 1855). Memories of Sport and Travel (Ludlow, England, 1938). Opens with a lively narrative of his service with the Hudson's Bay Co. in northern Canada in the seventies. 191

BURDEN, Harold Nelson (b. 1860). Life in Algoma (London 1894). Three years of clergyman's life as a missionary in Canada. Manitoulin (London 1895). Five years missionary work among Ojibway Indians and lumbermen. 192

BURN, Major-General Andrew (b. 1742). The Life of Andrew Burn (London, 1799). Service with Royal Marines, including service in American Revolution and in Canada. 193

BURNS, Rev. Robert (1789-1869 of Toronto). The Life and Times of the Rev. Robert Burns (Toronto, 1872).Includes an unfinished autobiography up to 1867; includes religious work in Toronto; Presbyterian theology; work at Knox College. 194

BURRISS, Rufus Allen. "Pioneering in New Ontario," in Canada Monthly XIII (1913). Settling in Rainy River district. 195

BURWELL, Col.Mahlon. Prisoner's diary,1814-1815; journey with Americans to Ohio and return on parole: comments on American places and on treatment of prisoners. MS, Light Papers, Ottawa Archives. 196

BUSKIN, George (born 1835). More than Forty Years in Gospel Harness (Berlin, Ont., 1898). Autobiography of a missionary and colporteur in England and Canada, mostly Northern Ontario. 197

BUTLAND, Ernest. Is Life Worth Living? (Montreal, 1918). Services with Canadian engineers, largely in China and France; mainly personal experiences. 198

BUTLER, Sir William Francis (1830-1910, soldier). The Great Lone Land (London, 1872). Travel and adventures in Canadian Northwest, 1870-1871; Red River rebellion. The Wild North Land (London, 1873). A winter journey with his dogs across Canada. Sir William Butler, An Autobiography (London,1911). His military career, including experiences in Canada during the Fenian raids and Red River expedition, and in the Canadian northwest. 199

BYNG, Marie Evelyn (Moreton), Viscountess (born 1870). Up the Stream of Time (Toronto, 1946). Living in Canada and other dominions with her soldier-husband; social life and public affairs. 200

BYRNES, John Maclay. The Paths of Yesterday (Boston, 1931). Memoirs of old St. John's, Newfoundland; nostalgic sketches of people, places, sport, customs, in the nineties. 201

CAMERON, Duncan. Fur-trader's journal, August-December 1804; with North West Company between Lake Superior and Hudson's Bay; travels and trade; rivalry with Hudson's Bay Company. L. R. Masson, Les Bourgeois de la Compagnie du Nord-Ouest (Quebec, 1889) II, 267-300. 202

CAMPBELL, Commander Andrew Bruce. Bring Yourself to an Anchor (London, 1941). Including his experiences as a trapper in Canada. 203

CAMPBELL, Bruce D. (b. 1913?). Where the High Winds Blow (New York, 1946). With the Hudson's Bay Company, 1934-1938; on Hudson Bay in New Quebec; Eskimo life. 204

CAMPBELL, Colin. Fur-trader's journals, 1828-1830, 1839-1840, 1841-1842; work as chief factor at Dunvegan post, Hudson's Bay Company. MS, Alberta Provincial Library, Edmonton. 205

CAMPBELL, Elizabeth Bethune. Where Angels Fear to Tread (Boston, 1940). Her legal experience in Canada and England; her fight for justice in a disputed will case; Ontario and London. 206

CAMPBELL, John Francis (1822-1885). Travel journal, July-November, 1864; adventures in Ontario and in Quebec; geological notes. A Short American Tramp (Edinburgh, 1865). 207

CAMPBELL, Patrick (d. 1823). Travel diary, June 1791-December 1792; a Scotsman in Quebec, Montreal, and St. John's; notes on farming, social life, politics, and topography. Travels in the Interior Inhabited Parts of North America (Edinburgh 1793); edited by H. H. Langton and W. F. Ganong (Toronto, 1937). 208

CAMPBELL, R. W. A Policeman from Eton (London, 1923). Service with North-West Mounted Police; travels and adventures; his colleagues and the ideals of the service. 209

CAMPBELL, Robert (1808-1894). Travel journal, November 1832-September 1833; a trip to Kentucky to buy sheep for the Red River colony. North Dakota Hist. Quar. I (1926) 35-45. Fur trading journal, 1848-1851; services with Hudson's Bay Company in western Canada; in Mackenzie River district; discovery of the Yukon River. MS (typed transcripts), Vancouver Public Library, Seattle Public Library, Toronto Public Libraries, University of Washington. A similar journal; an exploration of the Upper Stikine and the sources of the Yukon River. Canadian Magazine, XLV (1915). "From the Highlands to Fort Garry;" reminiscences of his life and labors in the service of the Hudson's Bay Company as chief factor,1830 to 1871." MS, Provincial Library, Victoria, 123 pp.; see also "A Fur Trader's Memoirs," Scottish Geog. Mag. L (1934) 147-155.   210

CAMPBELL, Roderick (born 1842). The Father of St. Kilda (London, 1901). Autobiography of a Scottish boy who went to the Hudson's Bay Company territory; experiences in charge of a fur-trading post in Northern Canada, 1859-1878.   211

CAMPBELL, Capt. William. Arctic Patrols (Milwaukee,1936). His service with the Royal Canadian Mounted Police; travels and adventure maintaining law and hunting down criminals in the Yukon and Arctic.   212

CAMPBELL, William Wilfred (1861-1918). Journal of a Canadian author. MS, Queen's University, Kingston, Ontario, in Lorne Pierce collection.   213

CANNELL, Kathleen. I Am Yesterday (New York,1945). Her family life in Port Hope, Canada, and across into U.S.A.; personal life.   214

CAPON, Peter, of Bordeaux. Sea journal, August-November 1715; at Annapolis,Cape Breton, investigating Indian depredations Hist. Mag., 3d Ser. III (1875), 18-20.   215

CARLETON. Public journal, July 1775-June 1776; account of the most remarkable events which happened in Canada. MS, Canadian Archives, Ottawa; MS, McGill University, D 32.   216

CARR, Emily (1871-1945), of Victoria, B.C. The Book of Small (Oxford, 1942). A fond record of her childhood and her family in Victoria. The House of All Sorts (Toronto, 1944).Feminine sketches of domestic concerns at her home in Victoria. Growing Pains (Toronto, 1946). Delicate sketches and reminiscences of her childhood, family; training as an artist and her work.   217

CARR, Lieut. George Kirwan, of Halifax. Travel diary, October December 1832;from Halifax to New York, Washington, and return; social life, manners, of U.S.A.: Fanny Kemble. Bull. New York Public Library XLI (1937), 743-774; MS, in New York Public Library.   218

CARR, William Guy (b. 1895). High and Dry (London, 1938). By Guess and by God (London, 1931). Adventures in Canada after World War I; farming, logging, hunting, building; merchant seaman, policeman; social life, politics, and principal happenings in Canada. 219

CARREL, F. Impressions of War (Quebec, 1919). Personal experience of service with Canadian troops in France during 1st World War. 220

CARROLL, John (1809-1884). My Boy Life (Toronto, 1882). Boyhood in Bay of Fundy district; education, Methodism, sport; life in Canadian wilderness. 221

CARROLL, Peter Owen. Life and Adventures (1924). Career as a detective; not seen; copy in Dennis College, Acadia University. 222

CARRUTHERS, John (died 1866). Retrospect of Thirty-Six Years' Residence in Canada West (Hamilton, 1861). Missionary journeys of a catechist and exhorter of the Church of Scotland; Upper Canada, mainly 1832-1861. 223

CARTER, W. J. (b. 1855, of Prince Albert). Reminiscences. MS, University of Saskatchewan, 339 pp. and typewritten copy in University of Toronto Library. Pioneer life in Saskatchewan, 1878-1919; Hudson's Bay Company; settlers; Riel rebellion, etc. 224

CARTLAND, J. Henry. Ten Years at Pemaquid (Pemaquid Beach, 1899). Notes on Acadian life, history, antiquities, border wars, etc. 225

CARTWRIGHT, Capt. George (1739-1819). Pioneer's diary, March 1770-October 1786; daily record of life and adventures during residence on Labrador coast; excellent details of pioneer life; topography, inhabitants, etc. Journal of Transactions and Events (Newark, 1792), 3 vols.; reprinted as Captain Cartwright and His Labrador Journal, ed. C.W. Townsend (Boston, 1911). 226

CARTWRIGHT, Mary Josephine. Family diary, June 1896-June 1900; family affairs; Liberal Party politics; events in the life of her father Sir Richard Cartwright, statesman. MS, Toronto Public Libraries, 2 vols. 227

CARTWRIGHT, Hon. Richard (1759-1815). Life and Letters, edited C. E. Cartwright (Toronto, 1876). American loyalist; exile in Kingston, where he was judge and legislator; law, public affairs, Indian activities, life of loyalists. 228

CARTWRIGHT, Sir Richard John (1835-1912). Reminiscences (Toronto,1912). His parliamentary and political life in Canada, 1863-1896; elections; Imperial relations; interviews. 229

CASH, Gwen. I Like British Columbia (Toronto, 1938). Twenty years of life in British Columbia; the general scene. 230

CASSAN, Matthew Sheffield. "Some Account of," Women's Canadian Hist. Soc. Toronto Trans. XXII (1923), 23-30. The journal of an Irish soldier who settled in Seymour, Ontario, in the year 1834. 231

CASSON, Herbert N. The Story of My Life (London, 1931). His career as leader of the Efficiency Movement; boyhood in Canada as son of Methodist missionary; industrial life; antisocialism; later in U.S.A. and England. 232

CHABERT, Joseph Bernard, Marquis de (1724-1805). Voyage Fait par Ordre du Roi en 1750 et 1751 (Paris, 1753). Abridgement of journal of a voyage made to rectify maps of Canada; with geographical observations. 233

CHAMBERS, Oswald (1874-1917). My Utmost for His Highest (Toronto, 1935). Religious life and work in Canada. 234

CHAPAIS, J. C. Réminiscences et Revendications (Quebec,1910). Not seen. 235

CHAPIN, Mrs. Adele le Bourgeois. Their Trackless Way (London, 1931). Canadian memories; not seen. 236

CHAPPELL, Benjamin. Private personal diary, January 1775-Dec. 1787; his notes on family, personal, and local affairs and events; in Prince Edward Island; Methodist life and labours. MS, Public Library, Charlottetown, P.E.I.; see Dalhousie Review IX (1930) 461-474. 237

CHAPPELL, Edward (1792-1861). Exploration journal, May-November 1814; Indian and Eskimo life. Narrative of a Voyage to Hudson's Bay (London, 1817). 238

CHARLESWORTH, Hector Willoughby (1872-1945). Candid Chronicles (Toronto, 1925) and More Candid Chronicles (Toronto, 1928). Reminiscences and sketches of pioneer life; childhood, education; journalist on The Empire; politics, writers, theatre, social life, in and around Toronto. 239

CHAUMONOT, Rev. Père Pierre-Joseph-Marie (d. 1649). Autobiographie (Paris, 1885). Jesuit missionary among Hurons; his boyhood, vocation, Indian wars, travels, missionary labors, spiritual life; early 17th Century. 240

CHEADLE, Dr. Walter Butler (1835-1910). Travel Journal, June 1862-March 1863; the "first" trans-Canadian tourist; travel notes, hunting, mines, topography. Journal of a Trip across Canada, ed. A.G. Doughty and G. Lanctot (Ottawa 1931). 241

CHESTER, Francis. Shot Full (London, 1938). Autobiography of a marijuana addict; criminal life; includes Canada. 242

CHINIQUY, Reverend Père Charles Pascal Telesphore (1809-1899). Fifty Years in the Church of Rome (Chicago, 1885). Autobiography of a Roman Catholic priest who became a Protestant: attacks on Catholic theology and practice; labors on behalf of the temperance movement in Canada; translated from French edition (Montreal, 1885). Mes Combats (Montreal, 1946) is very similar. 243

CHOLET, Pierre (born 1840). L'Enfant Perdu et Retrouvé (Mile-End, Q., 1887). Autobiography, re-written by J. B. Proulx, of a child stolen from his parents; life at sea; search for and discovery of his family. 244

CHOQUETTE, Hon. Philippe-Auguste (born 1854, of Montreal). Un Demi-Siècle de Vie Politique (Montreal, 1936). Impersonal reminiscences of political and legal affairs and personalities in Canada. 245

CHRISTIAN, Lieut. Col. Edgar Vernon (1908-1927). Unflinching (London, 1937). A Diary of exploration in Northwest Canada in 1926-27; Thelon Game Sanctuary to Hudson's Bay; hunting, trapping, personal. 246

CHRISTIE, William. Travel diary (no dates given); Fort Garry to Fort Simpson, Mackenzie River; by land, water, and dog-train; return to Carlton. MS, Alberta Provincial Library, Edmonton. 247

CHRISTMAS, Rev. Henry. The Emigrant Churchman in Canada (London, 1849), Two vols. An Anglican minister's account of his experiences; Montreal, Toronto, Hamilton; notes on general conditions and politics; advice to emigrants. 248

CHURCH, H. E. (born 1868). An Emigrant in the Canadian Northwest (London, 1929). To Toronto in 1886; homesteading; experiences in British Columbia; forty years' farming. 249

CHURCHILL, Charles. Memorials of a Missionary Life in Nova Scotia (London, 1845). A Methodist's travel and work; notes on social and economic conditions. 250

CHUTE, Arthur Hunt. The Real Front (New York, 1918). Record of his service and experience with the First Canadian Division in France, 1914-1917; Ypres, etc. 251

CLAIRAMBAULT. Travel journal, 1672-1674; narrative of journey to Canada. MS, Ottawa Archives, Clairambault 864. 252

CLARK, Col. John (b. 1783). "Memoirs," Ontario Hist. Society Papers VII (1906), 157-193. Reminiscences of early British settlements in Ontario. 253

CLARKE, Charles (1826-1909). Sixty Years in Upper Canada (Toronto, 1908). Life and work as clerk of the Ontario Legislature; political affairs; the Fenians; the Riel rebellion; social life. 254

CLAUS, (William? or Warren?). General diary, 1770-1824 (with large gaps); fruit-farming at Niagara, Ont.; notes on boats and steamers on rivers and lakes; relations with Indians as Agent and Executive Counsellor; arbitration and legal work; gardening and social life; includes accounts, letters, commonplace books, etc. MS, Ottawa Archives. 255

CLAY, John. My Recollections of Ontario (Chicago, 1918). His life at Brantford; farming; public life; and personalities; social life. 256

CLEGG, Howard. A Canuck in England (London, 1943). Day-by-day narrative of service in England with Canadian troops during World War II; Canadian Light Infantry, 1939-1940; national habits and character and their interaction. 257

CLEVELAND, Mary Frances (b. 1868?). Private diary, September-October 1882; written at the age of fourteen, when she was sick with malaria. MS, Toronto Public Libraries, 11 pages (typewritten copy). 258

CLINKER KNOCKER. Aye, Aye, Sir (London, 1938). Including his experiences as a naval reservist in Canada. 259

CLINKSKILL, James. Reminiscences of a pioneer in Saskatoon, 1882 to 1912; his work as merchant and mayor; the Saskatchewan rebellion. MS, University of Saskatchewan, 269 pp. 260

CLINT, Mabel Brown (b. 1874). Our Bit (Montreal, 1934). Memories of a Canadian nursing sister 1914-1919; hospitals in London, on Western Front, and at Lemnos;interesting details of her work; partly diary. 261

CLUNE, Frank. Try Anything Once (Sydney, 1933). Including his travel and odd jobs in Canada. 262

COCHIN, Louis (b. 1856). "Reminiscences," Canadian North-West Hist. Society Pubs. I, No. 2 (1927) 75 pp. His travels and work as missionary to the Cree Indians; prisoner during the rebellion of 1885. 263

COCKING, Matthew. Fur-trader's journal, June 1772-June 1773; factor at Fort York, Hudson's Bay Company; travel from York to the Blackfeet country; notes on trade, Indians, travels. Proc. and Trans. Royal Soc. Canada, 3d Ser. II (1908), Sec. II, 91-121. MS, Ottawa Archives. 264

COLEMAN, Francis (1813-1900). Travel diary, April-June, 1834? Atlantic crossing, journey to Darlington Township, in Upper Canada, by way of Ottawa River and Rideau Canal. MS,Toronto Public Libraries, 123 pp. 265

COLLINS, John. A Journal of My Visit to England, Ireland, and Scotland (St. John, 1877). A Copy at Dennis College, Acadia University; not seen. 266

COLLINSON, Capt. Sir Richard (1811-1883). Exploration journal January 1850-May 1855; scientific observations and travel conditions on expedition to Arctic in search of Franklin's ships. Journal of H.M.S. Enterprise (London, 1889). 267

COLLISON, Rev. William Henry (1847-1922). In the Wake of the War Canoe (London, 1915). Forty years' work among the Indians of northern British Columbia; missionary work, Indian life and customs, fur-traders and Hudson's Bay Company; his adventures and perils. 268

COLNETT, Capt.James (1755?-1806). Travel journal, April 1789-November 1791; from Plymouth, Devon, to Northwest coast of Canada aboard the "Argonaut"; trading expeditions;troubles with Spaniards. The Journal of James Colnett, edited F. W. Howay (Toronto, 1940). 269

COMEAU, Napoleon Alexander (1848-1923). Life and Sport on the North Shore of the Lower St.Lawrence and Gulf (Quebec 1909)

French edition (Quebec, 1945). Autobiography, mainly relating to fishing, trapping, birds, Indians. 270

CONANT, Thomas (1842-1905). Life in Canada (Toronto, 1903). Reminiscences of the life, struggles, and conditions of early settlers in Canada. 271

"CONNOR, Ralph" (pseud.of Charles William Gordon, 1860-1937). Postcript to Adventure (New York, 1938). Autobiography of Canadian novelist; notes on literature, Toronto University, 1st World War in France. 272

[CONNOR, Thomas]. Fur-trading journal, September 1804-April 1805; trading and work at posts on Snake River; daily work; Indian customs. Charles M. Gates, Five Fur-Traders of the Northwest (Minneapolis, 1933), 245-278. 273

COOKESLEY, Frederick John (1839-1867). Religious diary, April 1860-April 1867; missionary work and travel in Africa, Labrador and Canada. Memorial Sketch with Extracts from His Diary, ed. Rev. W. G. Cookesley (London, 1867). 274

COONEY, Robert (1800-1870). The Autobiography of a Wesleyan Missionary (Montreal, 1856). His conversion from Catholicism; travels and missionary work in Upper and Lower Canada; religious controversy. 275

COOPER, F. C. In the Canadian Bush (London, 1915). A railway engineer's experiences of construction work in Northern Ontario; camp life and work in 1909. 276

COPLESTON, Mrs. Edward. Canada (London, 1861). Reminiscences and sketches of life in the bush, farming, domestic labors; Upper Canada, from 1856. 277

[COPWAY, George]. The Life, History, and Travels, of Kah-ge-ga-gah-bowh (Albany, 1847). Autobiography of a young Ojibway chief; his conversion and Methodist missionary labours for twelve years; boyhood and early Indian life around Lake Ontario; interesting. 278

COWAN, C. L. The Trail of the Sky Pilot (Toronto, 1929). His life as a Scottish Presbyterian missionary in 1908-1928; in British Columbia, Kootenay, etc.; lives of the lumberjacks; religious college. 279

COWAN, Dr. William. Private diaries,1856-1867; details of medical work at Fort Garry.MS,Public Archives, Ottawa. 280

COWDELL, Thomas D. A Poetical Journal of a Tour (Dublin, 1901). From Canada to England, Wales, and Ireland; notes on countryside, religion, politics; and on the jubilee.   281

COWIE, Isaac. The Company of Adventurers (Toronto, 1913). In the service of the Hudson's Bay Company, 1867-1874; life of a fur-trader; prairies, buffaloes, trade, etc.   282

COWLEY, Mrs. A. T. "Lower Fort Garry in 1868," Beaver, CCLXV (1934), 39-41. Reminiscences of the daughter of the chief trader at Lower Fort Garry, Manitoba.   283

COX, Ross (1793-1853). Adventures on the Columbia River (London, 1831) 2 vols. Service with Pacific Fur Co. and Northwest Co., 1811-1817; fur-trade and Indians.   284

CRAGG-FARTHING, Rt. Rev. John (b. 1861). Recollections (n.p., 1945). Reminiscences of an American-born clergyman, who was ordained at London, Ont., and was Bishop of Montreal, 1909-1939; personal affairs and his life work. A copy in McGill University library.   285

CRAIG, John D. (born 1903). Danger is My Business (New York, 1938). Adventurous career; Canadian-born.   286

CRAIG, John Roderick (b. 1837). Ranching with Lords and Commons (Toronto, 1903). Cattle ranching in Alberta; development of the Oxley Range; twenty years work; big business and management.   287

CRAN, Mrs. Marion (Dudley) (b. 1879). A Woman in Canada (London, 1910). Experimental farming near Ottawa; poultry and fishing; travels in Rockies and in British Columbia; social life in Quebec.   288

CREIGHTON, William Black (1864-1946). Round 'bout Sun-up (Toronto, 1946). Memories of a boyhood in an Irish family on a pioneer farm in Ontario.   289

CRESPEL, Emmanuel (1703?-1773). Voyage en Canada (Frankfort, 1742; Amsterdam, 1757; Quebec, 1808, 1884). Voyage to Canada, shipwreck on Anticosta. Copy Bibliothèque St.Sulpice, Montreal.   290

CROCOMBE, Leonard Cecil. An Editor Goes West (London, 1938). The journalistic and holiday travels of the editor of "Tit-Bits" in Canada.   291

CROIL, James (1821-1916). Life of James Croil (Montreal,1918) Autobiography; education in Scotland; editor for the Canadian Presbyterian and the Record; travels and his work for the church in Canada, U.S.A., and Europe; union of Presbyterian churches in Canada; legislation; life and interests of Presbyterians in Canada; useful work. 292

CROMER, Ruby, Countess. Such Were These Years (London, 1937). Diplomatic and social life; includes her official life with her husband in Canada. 293

CROOKS, Hon. James. "Recollections of the War of 1814," Women's Canadian Hist. Soc., Toronto, Trans., XIII (1914);11-24; Niagara Hist. Soc. Pubs. XXVIII (1916) 28-41. Fighting on the Niagara frontier; battle of Queenston Heights. 294

CROSBY, Revd. Thomas (1840-1914). Among the An-ko-me-nums or Flathead Tribes of the Pacific Coast (Toronto, 1907). Up and Down the North Pacific Coast, by Canoe and Mission Ship (Toronto, 1914). His Experiences as a Methodist missionary among the Indians of British Columbia; from 1863 until his death; Port Simpson district; travel, native life and customs and stories; pioneering; religion; useful. 295

CROZIER, John Beattie (b.1849). My Inner Life (London, 1898). Autobiography and personal evolution; his life in Galt;boyhood; medical schools;alcohol and temperance; literary figures. 296

CURRIE, Emma Augusta (Harvey) (1829-1913). "Reminiscences," Niagara Hist. Soc. Pubs. XX (1911) 23-34. Her schooldays at Niagara-on-the-Lake; recollections of famous people. 297

CURRIE, John Allister (b.1866). The Red Watch (Toronto, 1916) With the 1st Canadian Division in France, World War I; the experiences of the 48th Highlanders and himself; only part autobiographical. 298

CURRIE, Margaret. Margaret Currie, Her Book (Toronto, 1924). Not seen. Since found to be essays, recipes, etc. 299

CURRY, Captain Frederic C. From the St. Lawrence to the Yser (London, 1916). With the first Canadian Division in France, 1915-1916; Ypres, Givenchy; personal experiences. 300

CURWOOD, James Oliver (1878-1927). Son of the Forests (New York, 1930). The Autobiography of the life and writings of the famous Canadian author; completed by D.A. Bryant. 301

CYNOSURIDIS, Alphonse. Mémoires d'un Vieux Garçon (Montreal, 1865). Not seen. 302

D'ALEYRAC, Jean Baptiste (born 1737). Aventures Militaires au XVIIIe Siècle, ed. Charles Coste (Paris, 1935). First half is an autobiography of military services, under Montcalm in Canada, 1754-1760; siege and surrender of Quebec; description of the country. Copy in Bibliothèque St. Sulpice. 303

DALL, William Healey (1845-1927). Travel journal, September 1866-September 1868; scientific expedition to Yukon Territory; Indian life. "Travels on the Yukon" in The Yukon Territory, intro. F.M. Trimmer (London, 1898) 1-242. 304

DAOUST, Sergeant Charles R., of Montreal. Cent-Vingt Jours de Service Actif (Montreal, 1886). A diary record of the services of the 65th Company in Northwestern Canada in the 1885 rebellion; Montreal to Calgary, Edmonton, Fort Saskatchewan, and return; somewhat impersonal. Copy at Harvard. 305

D'ARTIGUE, Jean. Six Years in the Canadian North-West (Toronto, 1882). Service in North-West Mounted Police, 1874-1880; Saskatchewan; Indian troubles; his travel, policing, social life; translated from French. 306

DARVEAU, Jacqueline. Travel journal, July-August, 1937; from Quebec to British Columbia and to Alaska. Randonnée au Pays des Totems (Quebec, 1938). 307

DASHWOOD, Richard Lewis. Chiploquorgan (Dublin, 1871). Military life and services with the 15th Regiment in Canada and Newfoundland, from 1862; natural history; sport. 308

DAUBENY, Charles Giles Bridle (1795-1867). Travel diary, July 1837-July 1838; travels of a professor of chemistry and botany; in Canada in 1837. Journal of a Tour through the United States and Canada (Oxford, 1843). 309

DAVENPORT, Major H. M. Life and Recollections (London, 1869). Includes Canadian travel, military service, and sport. 310

DAVIDSON, John. "Ten Years in a Prohibition Town," Macmillan's Mag., February 1904. Experiences and observations on local option in Fredericton, N.B.; law and liquor. 311

DAVIS, Mary Lee. Sourdough Gold (Boston, 1933). Reminiscences of her experiences and observations at Dawson and elsewhere in the Yukon and Klondyke during 1898, etc.; Canadian woman pioneer; extracts from diary. 312

DAVIS, Robert Hobart. Canada Cavalcade (London, 1937). Travels and experiences of Canadian public and social life; the western interior provinces, and eastern and maritime provinces. 313

DAWSON, Sir John William (1820-1899). Fifty Years of Work in Canada (London, 1901). Student life in Edinburgh; teaching in Scotland and Nova Scotia;principal of McGill University; science and scholarship; Royal Society; women's education; his research and publications. 314

DEANE, Capt. Richard Burton (b. 1848). Mounted Police Life in Canada (London, 1916). His service with the Mounties, 1883 to 1914; Regina, Lethbridge, Calgary; his adventures and travels; crime and the code; Riel trial. 315

DEASE, John Warren (died 1830). Fur-trader's journal, August-December, 1829; activities of chief trader of Hudson's Bay Company at Fort Vancouver. MS,Provincial Library, Victoria, 9 pp. 316

DE BAUGY, Chevalier. Military diary, 1687; expedition of the Governor of New France against the Indians. Journal d'une Expédition contre les Iroquois (Paris, 1883); The Rochester Hist. Soc. Pubs., IX (1930) 3-56. 317

DE BOILEAU, Lambert. Recollections of Labrador Life (London, 1861). Pioneer life and conditions; Eskimo; animals; social life. 318

DE BRÉBEUF, Jean (1593-1649). Travels and Sufferings (London, 1938).Experiences and hardships of a Jesuit father and missionary among the Hurons of Canada; an autobiographical account, translated from French. 319

DE BOUGAINVILLE, Monsieur. Military journal, 1756-1768; kept while he was aide-de-camp to Montcalm; expedition to Canada and campaign there; siege of Quebec. Rapport de l'Archiviste...de Québec (Quebec, 1923) 202-393. 320

DE FIEDMONT, Jacau, of Louisbourg. Military journal, March-June, 1755; the siege of Beauséjour; with French artillery; translated from French. J.C. Webster, The Siege of Beauséjour in 1755 (New Brunswick Museum, 1936). 321

DE GASPÉ, Philippe Aubert (1786-1871). Mémoires (Ottawa 1866).

An autobiography of a French settler in Quebec; seigneur of St. Jean, Port Joli, L.C.; traditions and customs; life of Canadian aristocracy; frank account of his friends, society and events in Quebec in early 19th Century. 322

D'EGVILLE, Alan Hervey (born 1890).Adventures in Safety (London, 1937). Includes travel and skiing in Canada. 323

DE LA CHAUME, Henri. Terre-Neuve et les Terre-Neuviennes (Paris, 1886). Personal narrative of a year and a half spent in Newfoundland and Canada. 324

DE LA CORNE, St. Luc (1712-1784). Journal de Voyage de M. St. Luc de La Corne (Montreal, 1778). Account of his travels in Canada. Copy in Bibliothèque St. Sulpice. 325

DELAFOSSE, Frederick M. (Roger Vardon, pseud). English Bloods (Ottawa, 1930). A young Englishman learning pioneer farming in Muskoka District, Ont., 1878-1881. 326

DE LA PAUSE, Chevalier. Military journals, 1756-1760; personal narrative of his activities while serving under Montcalm in Canada. MS, Public Archives, Ottawa. 327

DE LA VÉRENDRYE,Pierre Gaultier de Varennes,Sieur (1685-1749) Travel journals, October 1730-September 1749; explorations for discovery of a western sea route. Journals,edited L. J. Burpee (Champlain Soc., Toronto, 1927). 328

DE LÉRY, Lieut. J. G. C. (1721-1797). Military journal, March 1754-April 1755; Quebec to Detroit; marches, topography,and Indians; by a Quebec engineer. Original text in Rapport de l'Archiviste de..Québec, 1928-1929; ed. by S.K. Stevens and D. H. Kent (Harrisburg, Pa., 1940). 329

DE LÉVIS, F. G., Maréchal. Military journal, 1756-1760;account of the campaign in Canada; siege of Quebec. H.R. Gasgrain, Guerre du Canada (Quebec, 1889), Vol. I. Journal de Mes Campagnes (Montreal, 1889). 330

DE LORIMER, Monsieur. Autobiographical account of his military service during the American invasion of Canada in 1775. H. A. Verreau (ed.), Invasion du Canada (Montreal, 1871)pp. 245-298. 331

DE MARTIGNY, Paul, of Montreal. Mémoires d'un Reporter (Montreal, n.d.); Les Mémoires d'un Garnement (Montreal, 1947). Journalistic reminiscences of people, events, and places;

his childhood in Canada; his work as a reporter. Copies in
Montreal Public Library, Collection Gagnon.   332

DE MONTREUIL, Chevalier. Military journal, August-September,
1755; battle of Lake George; translated from French. E. B.
O'Callaghan, Docs. Rel. Col. Hist. State New York, X (1858)
335-337.   333

DENISON, Col. George Taylor (1839-1925, of Toronto). Soldier-
ing in Canada (Toronto, 1900). His forty-five years in the
Canadian militia; a bodyguard to Governor-General; Fenians;
Northwest rebellion; trip to Russia. Struggle for Imperial
Unity (London, 1909). Political and military recollections
and experiences. Recollections of a Police Magistrate (Toronto, 1920). Court work, methods, personalities, in Toronto, from 1877 to 1919. See also his compilation, Reminiscences of the Red River Rebellion of 1869 (Toronto, 1873?); it
includes reminiscences by participants and witnesses.   334

DENISON, Gen. Septimus Julius Augustus (1859-1937). Memoirs
(Toronto, 1927). Schooling in Canada; military education in
England; service in Canadian army; Boer War; an A. D. C. in
World War I.   335

DE RAMEZAY, Sieur. Mémoire (Quebec, 1861,1927). Siege of Quebec and surrender; military and personal narrative; written
by the French commandant at Quebec. Copy at Laval University.   336

D'ERES, Charles Dennis Rusoe (born 1761, of Quebec). Memoirs
(Exeter, 1800). Canadian's capture during American Revolution; eleven years with Indians; journeys, sufferings, escape; Indian customs; Quebec area. Pamphlet in Ottawa Archives.   337

DE ST. MESMIN, Ferret. Travel journal, 1793; from England to
Halifax and on to Quebec, Montreal, and New York. MS, Ottawa Archives, 25-4-B.   338

DESILETS, Alfred, of Trois Rivieres. Souvenirs d'un Octogén-
aire (Trois Rivieres, Q., 1922). Mostly impersonal historical reminiscences of events and persons, at Trois Rivieres;
navigation, trade, religion. Copy at Bibliothèque St. Sulpice.   339

DES RIVIÈRES, Francis W., of Montreal. Personal diaries, September 1843-December 1872; family affairs; Catholic mission
work; farming, sawmills, deerhunting, weather; visits into

Montreal; partly in English, partly in French. MS, McGill University, D. 28, six vols. 340

DES VOEUX, Sir George William (1834-1909). My Colonial Service (London, 1903) 2 vols. Includes section on his governmental service in Newfoundland. 341

DETLOR, George Hill (b. 1794, of Kingston, Ont.). Private diary, September 1851-December 1862; notes on social affairs; work as a coroner, notary public, arbitrator, and councillor: religion, weather, etc. MS, owned by Mrs. E. A. Dey, of London, Ontario; typed copy at Queen's University, which also has a copy of his "Historical Recollections," containing lists of friends, deaths, events, memoirs, etc. 342

DE TROYES, Pierre chevalier (d.1688). Military diary, March-August, 1686; expedition overland from Montreal to Hudson's Bay to retake forts. Journal de l'Expédition du Chevalier de Troyes (Beauceville, Que., 1918). Copy in Toronto Public Libraries. 343

DE TURENNE, Louis, comte. Travel diary, October 1875-December 1876; notes on people, places, and personal experiences in United States and Canada. Quatorze Mois dans l'Amérique du Nord (Paris, 1879) 2 vols. 344

DE VAUDREUIL, Monsieur. Sea journal, May-June, 1755; with the French fleet under De la Mothe from Brest to Quebec; translated. E.B. O'Callaghan, Docs. Rel. Col. Hist. State of New York, X (1858) 297-299. 345

DE VERNEUIL, Monsieur. Croquis de Guerre, 1915-1917 (Montreal 1921). Personal military experiences; in the Western Front with Canadian forces; World War I. 346

DEVILLEBON, Joseph Robineau. Acadia at the End of the Seventeenth Century, by John C. Webster (St. John, 1934) has the journals kept by this commandant in Acadia, 1690-1700. 347

DE VILLIERS, Neyon. Military journal, July, 1754; account of the defeat of the British at the Beautiful River; translated from French. E. B. O'Callaghan, Docs. Rel. Col. Hist. of State New York, X (1858) 261-262. 348

DEWAR, Neil (b. 1793). Narrative of the Shipwreck and Sufferings (Greenock, 1820?). Very brief autobiography of a seaman, who lost both legs and arms after the wreck of the Rebecca of Quebec off the coast of Labrador in 1816. 349

DEWDNEY, Edgar (1835-1916). Private diary, 1859; contents unknown. MS, Provincial Library, Victoria, 37 pp. (typewritten copy). 350

DICKENS, Francis (1844-1886).Diary of Francis Dickens, edited V. La Chance (Kingston, Ont., 1930). An Inspector in North-West Mounted Police; troubles with Indians; attacks on Fort Pitt, Sask., in 1885. See also, Queen's Quar. XXXVII (1930) 312-334. 351

[DICKIE, G. H.]. Out of the Past: by An M.P. (1934). Autobiography from the eighties; varied jobs as hotel keeper and miner in British Columbia; M.P. in British Columbia legislature; anecdotes of the West and of a varied career. 352

DIGBY, Lieut. William. Military journal, April 1776-October 1777; with a Shropshire Regiment to Canada under Burgoyne; campaigns; the battle of Hilberton. J. P. Baxter (ed.), The British Invasion from the North (Albany, 1887) 412 pp. 353

DILL, W. S. The Long Day (Ottawa, 1926). Reminiscences of the Yukon; sketches of amusing events and people; the gold-rush scene. 354

DINESEN, Thomas. Merry Hell (London,1931). Personal narrative of a Danish V.C. who trained and served in World War I with the Canadian Black Watch; a simple and frank tale. 355

DONKIN, John G. Trooper and Redskin in the Far North-West (London, 1889). With the North-West Mounted Police in 1884-1888; travels, crimes, trappers, hunters, Indians. 356

DORAN, George Henry (b. 1869). Chronicles of Barabbas, 1884-1934 (Toronto, 1935). The reminiscences of a Canadian-born writer and publisher, who went to the United States when he was 21; short section on his youth. 357

DORLAND, John T. (1860-1896, of Wellington, Ontario). Quaker diary, April 1888-May 1895; travel and ministry,Canada and Palestine. W.K.Baker,John T. Dorland (London, 1898). 358

DORWIN, J.H. (born 1792, of Montreal). Private diary, March 1811-November 1883; preceded by an autobiography of boyhood in Vermont; early removal to western New York; then to Montreal in 1815; a trader and merchant there; Canadian business; people, towns, buildings, and history. A very detailed record, by a very curious man; most valuable for the Quebec scene, events, changes, rumours; and similar material relating to his travels in Newfoundland, Labrador, and Ontario; also American news, and notes on science and meteorology; a most valuable record. MS, Ottawa Archives, 8 vols. 359

DOUGLAS, David (1798-1834). Travel journals, 1824-1834; two trips to the Pacific North-West; Columbia, Red River, York Factory; on behalf of Horticultural Society of London. Companion to the Botanical Magazine (London) II(1835-1836) 79-182; Oregon Hist. Soc. Quar. VI (1905); Journal Kept by David Douglas (London, 1914), 364 pp. 360

DOUGLAS, Lieut. J. Harvey. Captured (New York, 1918). Canadian soldier's experiences in 1st World War; capture and imprisonment in Germany; hospitals; release. 361

DOUGLAS, James (1800-1886, of Quebec). Medical diary, March-July, 1818; notes of a surgeon on a whaling ship; also his reminiscences of his medical studies and practice in Canada. Journals and Reminiscences, edited by J. Douglas (New York, 1910). 362

DOWNES, Prentice Gilbert (b. 1909). Sleeping Island (New York 1943). Travel and fishing in the barren lands of the Canadian Far North. 363

DRESSLER, Marie (b. 1871?). My Own Story (Boston, 1934). Includes section on her childhood in Coburg, Ont. 364

DREW, Benjamin (ed.). The Refugee, or the Narratives of Fugitive Slaves in Canada (Boston,1856). Short autobiographical stories by a large number of American negro slaves, who escaped into Canada. 365

DRISCOLL, Frederick (b. 1830). "Memoirs of a Canadian," Montreal Gazette, 1860. Reminiscences of a Canadian journalist; foreign correspondent for Canadian and American newspapers; American Civil War; sports. 366

DROLET, Gustave A., of Montreal. Zouaviana (Montreal, 1898). Happy memories, 1868-1898; journeys to Europe; his studies; services as sergeant in Zouaves Pontificales; political affairs in Quebec; French-Canadian celebrities and religious life. 367

DUCHARME, Léandre (born 1816?). Journal of a Political Exile (Sydney, 1944): originally published as, Journal d'une Expédition Politique aux Terres Australes (Montreal,1845). On his part in the 1838 rebellion in Canada; his imprisonment and exile; settlements and settlers in Australia. 368

DUFFERIN AND AVA, Frederick Temple-Hamilton-Temple-Blackwood, 1st Marquis of (1826-1902). Travel diary, July-October 1876; informal account of journey from Ottawa to British Columbia and back. <u>Journal of the Journey of His Excellency the Governor-General of Canada</u> (London, 1877) 369

DUFFERIN AND AVA, Hariot, Marchioness of (1843-1936). Social diary, June 1872-August 1877; a personal record of travels, society, and official life, work, and ceremonies, and domestic affairs, kept while her husband was Governor-General. <u>My Canadian Journal</u> (London, 1891). 370

DUFFIELD, Alexander James. <u>Recollections of Travels Abroad</u> (London, 1889). Including a section on travel and mining in Canada. 371

DUNCAN, Eric (**born** 1858). <u>From Shetland to Vancouver Island</u> (Edinburgh, 1937). Farming as a boy in Shetlands; Vancouver from 1877; farms, frontier, religion, schools, churches, social; covers 75 years. 372

DUNCAN, Francis (1836-1888). <u>Our Garrisons in the West</u> (London, 1864). Reminiscences of six years' military service in British America; description of towns and areas. 373

DUNDONALD, Earl of (<u>b</u>. 1852). <u>My Army Life</u> (London, 1926). It includes a section on his military service in Canada. 374

DUNLOP, Dr. William (1792-1848). <u>Recollections of the American War</u> (Toronto, 1908). A Scotsman's service with the Connaught Rangers in Upper Canada, 1812-1814; military activities and personal details. 375

DURAND, Charles (1811-1905, of Toronto). <u>The Reminiscences of Charles Durand</u> (Toronto, 1897). Details of 1837 rebellion; his imprisonment; war and politics; his work as a barrister; legal practice and politics in Ontario; up to 1860. 376

DURHAM, Louisa Elizabeth (Grey) Lambton, Countess of (1797?-1841). Private diary, April-December 1838; her private and public life; travels in Canada; occurrences during her husband's term as Governor-in-Chief of British North America, after the 1837 rebellion. <u>Lit. Hist. Soc. Quebec</u>, Series 9 (1915) 3-61. 377

DWIGHT, Charles P. (1872-1901). <u>Life in the North-West Mounted Police</u> (Toronto 1892). Experiences of a new recruit during six months in the service; personal details. 378

DYKER, Bob. Get Your Man (London, 1934). Personal adventures during his service with North-West Mounted Police, 1907-14; romantic life and loves; badmen and strange characters. 379

DYOTT, General William (1761-1847).Military journal, February 1781-April 1845; including army service in Canada. Dyott's Diary (London, 1907), 2 vols. 380

EARLE, Mrs. C. W. Memoirs and Memories (London, 1911). Her marriage and domestic life in Canada. 381

EASTBURNE, Robert (born 1710). The Dangers and Sufferings of Robert Eastburne (Cleveland, 1904). His capture by Indians; experiences in Montreal areas; sufferings; deliverance. 382

EATON, Evelyn Sybil Mary (b. 1902). Every Month Was May (New York, 1946); The North Star is Nearer (New York, 1949). Her nostalgic reminiscence of light-hearted episodes of life in Paris, London, and various other parts of the world, in the twenties and thirties; New Yorker articles. 383

EDGAR, Helen Madeline (Boulton). Dahabeah Days (Toronto,1923) Her diary of an Egyptian winter holiday in a house-boat on the Nile. 384

ELGIN HISTORICAL AND SCIENTIFIC INSTITUTE. Reminiscences of Early Settlers (St. Thomas, Ont., 1911). Includes reminiscences of George Munro, Sheriff McKellar, George Kerr, Roswell Tomlinson (1837 rebellion),Samuel Williams(1837 rebellion), and A. W. Graham (Red River rebellion). 385

ELIOT, Elinor Marsden. My Canada (London, 1915). An English girl trying ranch life in Western Canada; earlier twentieth century. 386

ELKINGTON, W. M. Five Years in Canada (London, 1895). Experiences and difficulties of wheat farming in Manitoba, 1889-1894. 387

ELLICE, Janie. Travel diary, April 1838-December 1838; from England to Quebec, Montreal, Niagara,and return; her social life; held prisoner in rebellion; relative of Edward Ellice the fur-trader of Montreal. MS, Ottawa Archives. 388

ELLIOTT, Sizar. Fifty Years of Colonial Life (Melbourne,1887) Boyhood in New Brunswick, in and about St. John; apprentice to merchant; emigration to Australia. 389

ELLIS, William Hodgson. "The Adventures of a Prisoner of War" Canadian Mag., July, 1899. Experiences as a captive of the Fenian invaders of Canada in 1866. 390

ANON. An Emigrant's Journal: Adventures in Canada (London, 1851). His wretched experiences on Lake Tobique, New Brunswich; warnings to intending emigrants. Copy in Bibliothèque St. Sulpice. 391

ENGLEHEART, Sir John Gardner Dillman (1823-1923). Travel diary, July-November, 1860; private secretary on the Prince of Wales' journey through Canada and America; official society life. Journal of the Progress of H. R. H. Prince of Wales (London, 1860). 392

ERMATINGER, Edward (1797-1876). Fur-trading journal, March 1827-October 1828; at York Factory, Hudson's Bay Company; journeys between Vancouver and Hudson's Bay; hunting, weather, trade. Royal Soc. Canada Proc. and Trans. 3d Ser. VI (1912) Sec. II, 67-127. 393

ERMATINGER, Frank (1798-1857). Military journal, June-July, 1828; expedition against the Indians of Puget Sound. Washington Hist. Quar. I (1907) 16-29. 394

ESMONDE, Sir T. H. Grattan. Hunting Memories of Many Lands (London, 1925). Includes section on travel and shooting in Canada. 395

EVANS, Henry (1725?-1782, of Annapolis). Travel diary, April-November 1760; a judge's voyage from Marblehead to Halifax; business affairs. W.A. Calnek, History of the County of Annapolis (Toronto, 1897), 148-151. 396

EVANS, Rev. James (1801-1846, of Hull). Religious journals, 1840-1842 (extracts); missionary work among Indians in Saskatchewan; work on his Indian alphabet; fur-traders. Egerton R. Young, The Apostle of the North (Toronto, 1900), 197-224. 397

EVANS, R. C. (born 1861). Autobiography (London, Ont., 1907). His life from his boyhood in Quebec and Ontario; a minister and elder of Mormon church; travel and evangelism. 398

EVANS, Richard Jones (1818-1888). His Memoirs written in 1868; youth in Ireland; emigration to Canada, life in London and Goderich districts, Ont. MS, Toronto Public Libraries, 49 pp. (typewritten copy). 399

EYRE-WALKER, B. Rolling on (London, 1936). Travel and work from early 20th Century; on a Western Canadian ranch, a firm in Virginia; and in New Zealand; in Canada he describes his experiences of cowboys and the tough life; humorous. 400

FAIRCLOUGH, Henry Rushton (1862-1938). Warming Both Hands (Palo Alto, California, 1941). A Canadian's autobiography; including service with Red Cross in Switzerland and Montenegro. 401

FAITHFULL, Lilian M. (born 1865). The Evening Crowns the Day (London, 1940). Life of a social worker; includes two chapters on travel and work in Canada. 402

FANE, Lady Augusta Fanny. Chit Chat (London, 1926). Includes a section on travel and sport in Canada. 403

FARAUD, Mgr. Henri (b. 1823). Dix-Huit Ans chez les Sauvages: par Fernand-Michel (Paris, 1870). Autobiography of a French missionary to Indians in far North of Canada, 1846-1864; in Hudson's Bay and Peace River region; Indian customs; Bishop of Anemour. Copy at Harvard. 404

FARIES, Hugh (1779-1852). Fur-trading journal, July 1804-May 1805; trade around Rainy Lake post, North-West Company; his work and social life. Charles M. Gates, Five Fur-Traders of the Northwest (Minneapolis, 1933) 189-241. 405

ANON, Farming in the Canadian North-West: by Old Farmer (London, 1906). Narrative of his experiences farming on the Manitoba prairies. 406

FAUGHNAN, Thomas. Stirring Incidents in the Life of a British Soldier (Picton, Ont., 1888). After his career in the army, emigrated to Canada and settled at Picton; life there. 407

FAWCETT, Edgar (b. 1847). Some Reminiscences of Old Victoria (Toronto, 1912). British Columbia fifty years before; pioneer life and conditions in Victoria; local personalities; originally newspaper articles. 408

FEILD, Right Rev. Edward (1801-1876, Bishop of Newfoundland). Religious diaries, 1845, 1846, 1849; on visitation journeys to missions on the coast of Newfoundland. The Church in the Colonies: Diocese of Newfoundland, Nos. 10, 15, 25 (1846 to 1850). 409

FEILD, P. A Sojourn in Canada(Stratford-upon-Avon 1912). Not seen. 410

FERLAND, l'Abbé J. B. E. (1805-1864). Travel journal, June to August, 1836; travel on Gaspé peninsula; topography, villages, fishermen, customs, etc. La Gaspésie (Quebec, 1877). copy in Bibliothèque St. Sulpice. 411

FERRIER, Alexander David (1813-1890). Early Days of Fergus (Guelph, 1866; Fergus, 1923). Three lectures on Canada from times when he arrived, in 1830 and later; life and trade in Montreal and Quebec; farming and early settlements, schools and politics in Fergus. Pamphlet in Ottawa Archives. 412

FIDLER, Isaac. Observations on Professions, Literature, Manners and Emigration in the United States and Canada (London 1833). Autobiography of a clergyman's search for employment together with sociological observations, 1831-1832. 413

FIDLER, Peter (1769-1822). Travel diary, September 1791-April 1792; with Indians to Slave Lake and River; Indian affairs, life, and customs; fur-trading. Journals of Samuel Hearne and Philip Turnor (Toronto, 1934) 493-555. 414

FIELD, Mrs. Edith (Coventry) (born 1864). The Good Old Days (Detroit, 1938). Narrative of her life pioneering and farming in Ontario. 415

FINAN, P. Travel journal, April-August 1825; to Quebec; recollections of Canada during the war of 1812; Journal of a Voyage to Quebec (Newry, Mass., 1828). 416

[FINLAY, Hugh?]. Military journal, November 1775-May 1776; a running commentary on the siege of Quebec; military and personal details. Lit. Hist. Soc. Quebec, Hist. Docs. 4th Ser. (1875) 25 pp. 417

FISHER, Alexander (d.1838). Exploration journal, April-November, 1818; to Davis Strait and Baffin's Bay; Eskimo customs. Journal of a Voyage of Discovery to the Arctic Regions (London, 1820). Exploration journal, May 1819-October 1820; travel in the Canadian Arctic. A Journal of a Voyage of Discovery to the Arctic Regions (London, 1821). 418

FISHER, James (b.1836). Life and Travels of James Fisher (Toronto, 1890). Army career; later part deals with his service in New Brunswick and Toronto. 419

FITZGIBBON, James (1780-1863). Military reminiscences, October-December, 1837; occurrences in Toronto during the 1837 rebellion. MS, Toronto Public Libraries, 20 pp. 420

FITZGIBBON, Mary Agnes (1851-1915). A Trip to Manitoba (London, 1880). Her homely adventures during a year and a half spent in Manitoba; social life in early Winnipeg. 421

FITZPATRICK, Frank Joseph Emile (b. 1861). Sergeant 331 (New York, 1921). Personal recollections of his service with the North-West Mounted Police in 1889-1895; adventures, crimes, Indians. 422

FLEMING, Sir Sandford (1827-1915, of Toronto). Private diary, 1854-1899; cryptic records of his travel and business as a railway engineer; surveying, engagements, payments; public engagements; meetings with Canadian celebrities; mostly of biographical value; also accounts and note-books. MS, Ottawa Archives, 8 boxes. 423

FLETCHER, Edward Taylor (1816-1897). "Reminiscences of old Quebec," Canadian Antiq. X (1913), 103-169. Quebec City in 1827-1881; schooldays, politics, social life. 424

FORSTER, John Wycliffe Lowes (1850-1938). Under the Studio Light (Toronto, 1928). A Canadian painter's reminiscences from the seventies; study in England and Europe; painters there; the public men he painted. 425

FOSTER, Sir George Eulas (1847-1931). Public diaries, February 1913-September 1929; tours in Australia, France, England; the battlefields; Peace conferences; League of Nations meetings in Geneva. W. Stewart Wallace, Memoirs of Sir George Foster (Toronto, 1933). 426

FOUCHER, Antoine. War journal, 1775; kept during the siege of Fort St. Jean; by the notary of Montreal; a detailed record. Bulletin des Recherches Historiques, XL (1934) pp. 135-159, 197-222. 427

FOUNTAIN, Paul. The Great North-West and the Great Lake Region of North America (London, 1904). Personal experiences in western Canada and the United States thro' many years, from 1865; fishing, lumbering, wilderness life. See also, "Canada in the Sixties," Longman's Mag., XLII (July, 1903) 237-250. His experiences as a young man, hunting and trapping in the head-waters of the Ottawa River with Indians. 428

FOURNIER, Jules. Souvenirs de Prison (Montreal, 1910). A copy in Dennis College, Acadia University; not seen. 429

FOWLER, Thomas. Travel journal, 1831; Englishman's tour thro' Canada to Niagara; topography, towns, customs. The Journal of a Tour through British America (Aberdeen, 1832). 430

FRANCHÈRE, Gabriel (1786-1863). Travel journal, 1810-1914; a voyage to the Northwest coast of Canada. MS, Toronto Public Libraries; first published from this copy (Montreal, 1820); translated and published by Redfield (New York, 1854): this was the basis for Washington Irving's Astoria. 431

FRANQUET, Louis (1697-1768). Settler's journal, July-August, 1752; and February-March, 1753; settlement and social life along the St.Lawrence and Richelieu Rivers. Voyages et Mémoires sur le Canada (Quebec, 1889). 432

FRASER, Donald (1826-1892). Autobiography (London, 1892). His early life and work as Presbyterian minister in Canada from 1851 to 1859; and in Great Britain; sermons. 433

FRASER, H. L. "Breaking Trail in the Sub-Arctic," Blackwood's Mag. CCXXII (1927) 752-765. Account of experiences during a winter patrol with the North-West Mounted Police. 434

[FRASER, Joshua]. Shanty, Forest and River Life in the Backwoods of Canada (Montreal, 1883). Experiences and observations of pioneer life, hunting, trapping, and lumbering in Ontario. 435

FRASER, Col. Malcolm (1733-1815). Military journal, May 1759-May 1760; services at siege of Quebec; full descriptions of military operations. Lit. Hist. Soc. Quebec, Hist. Docs. 2d Series (1927) 1-37; Journal Society Army Hist Research XVIII, (1939) 135-168. 436

FRASER, Simon (1776-1862). Travel diary, April-July, 1806; a first exploration of the Fraser River; fur-trading. Report Public Archives (Ottawa, 1930) pp. 109-145. Travel journal, May-August 1808; from the Rockies to the Pacific;fur-trade. MS,Toronto Public Libraries; published with various changes in L.R. Masson, Les Bourgeois de la Compagnie du Nord-Ouest (Quebec, 1889-1890) I, Pt. 2, 166-221. 437

FRASER, Rev. William (born 1808). Clergyman's journal, August 1834-July 1835; ordination in Pictou County, N. S.; settlement in Bond Head, Simcoe County, U. C.; early Presbyterian life and work; travel, visits, parish affairs and religious reflections, etc.; entertaining and useful. London and Middlesex Hist. Soc. Trans. XIV (1930) 80-156.   438

FRENCH, Lieut.G. Exploration journal, September-October 1783; along the Ottawa River, from Carillon to Rideau, and to the source; thence to St.Lawrence; notes on timber. Report Canadian Archives 1890 (Ottawa, 1891) 67-70.   439

FRESHMAN, Rev. Charles (b.1819). Autobiography (Toronto 1868) Education in Germany; his work as a rabbi;conversion to Methodism; his life and work among Methodists in Germany and in Ontario; Preston and Quebec.   440

FRIPP, Edward Fitz-Gerald. The Outcasts of Canada (Edinburgh, 1932).Experiences of an English immigrant in British Columbia in the twenties.   441

FRITH, Dean (pseud.). Booze-Runner (London, 1935). Experience while runner of liquor over the American border in the prohibition era; Quebec; capture, imprisonment; life with the tough set.   442

FROBISHER, Joseph. Private diary. MS, McGill University.Not seen.   443

FROST, Rev. F. Sketches of Indian Life (Toronto, 1904). His thirty years' work as missionary among Indians; Ojibways of northern shores of Huron and Superior; Garden River; Manitoulin Island; an attractive account of Indian life and customs.   444

FROST, Sarah (Scofield). Travel diary, May-June, 1783; a woman loyalist's journey from Long Island to St.John River, in what is now New Brunswick. Walter Bates, Kingston and the Loyalists of...1783 (St. John, N. B., 1889) 26-30.   445

GAGNON, Blanche. Réminiscences et Actualités (Quebec, 1939). People and places; little personal.   446

GAGNON, Hélène J. Blanc et Noir (Montreal, 1944). Travels in Europe and Africa during World War II.   447

GALLISHAW, John. Trenching at Gallipolli (Toronto, 1916). The personal experiences of a Newfoundland soldier in World War I; Dardanelles expedition; life in dug-outs.   448

GALLOWAY, Margaret A. I Lived in Paradise (Winnipeg, 1941).

Family history of her years in a Manitoba village, in late 19th Century; Scotch Presbyterian community. 449

GALT, John (1779-1839). Autobiography (Philadelphia, 1833), 2 vols. Includes long section on his travels and labours in Canada, settling claims for the sufferers from War of 1812; in Ontario; founding of Guelph; business of the Canada Company; settlers, people, weather, conditions. 450

GANDIER, A. "Experience of a Canadian Pastor," International Rev. Miss. III (1914). Missionary work and travel. 451

GAPPER, Mary Sophia (O'Brien) (1798-1876). Pioneering diary, 1828-1838; emigration and settlement at Shanty Bay, on Lake Simcoe; experiences of farming and pioneering life in Upper Canada. MS, Public Archives, Toronto, 440 pp. 452

GARDINER, Richard (1723-1781). Memoirs of the Siege of Quebec (London, 1761); reprinted in Doughty's The Siege of Quebec. Military details of the siege by a captain of militia. 453

GARLAND, Bessie (Ford). The Old Man's Darling (Toronto, 1881) An autobiographical account of her childhood and early life in Ireland, and of her experiences while an emigrant in Canada. 454

GARNEAU, François-Xavier (1809-1866). Voyage en Angleterre et en France (Quebec, 1835). Travel experiences and descriptions, 1831-1833; the book was suppressed; a copy is in the Bibliothèque St. Sulpice, Montreal. 455

GARRIOCH, Alfred Campbell (b. 1848). A Hatchet Mark in Duplicate (Toronto, 1929). An Autobiography of a long career as a missionary and teacher among the Indians of the Peace River country. 456

GARRY, Nicholas (1782?-1856). Travel journal, March-November, 1821; England to New York to Montreal, journeys to Hudson's Bay Company posts in the North-West, and back; his descriptions and notes on business, topography, and social life by the Deputy-Governor. Royal Soc. Canada Proc. and Trans. 2d Series VI (1900), Sec. II, 73-204; see also, Beaver, CCLXI, (1931). 457

GATES, William. Recollections of Life in Van Dieman's Land (Lockport, 1850). An Autobiography of a Canadian patriot of 1837; transported to Tasmania; details of the country, station life; his activities as overseer and policeman. 458

GEIKIE, George Cunningham (1824-1906). <u>Life in the Woods</u> (London, 1874). Account of his boyhood, farming and settling in the Canadian bush; bush preaching and religion; social life and ideas in Upper Canada. 459

GEIKIE, John C. (editor). <u>Adventures in Canada</u> (Philadelphia, 1882?). A narrative of homesteading, farming, general life in Niagara and Ontario. 460

GERIN-LAJOIE, A. <u>Dix Ans au Canada, 1840-1850</u> (Quebec, 1888). Not seen. Since found to be history only. 461

GIBBONS, Sergt. Arthur. <u>A Guest of the Kaiser</u>(Toronto, 1919). Personal narrative of a Canadian Soldier's experiences as a prisoner-of-war in Germany during World War I. 462

GIBSON, James. <u>A Journal of the Late Siege</u> (London, 1745). A day-to-day account of the naval siege of Louisbourg; pamphlet in Ottawa Archives. 463

GIBSON, William J. <u>Wild Career</u> (London, 1935). A Canadian's crowded years of adventure in Russia and the near East; his service in Russian army during World War I; the Revolution; work as commissar; arrest by the Cheka. 464

GILBERT, George (1754?-1781). Exploration journal, 1776-1780; narrative of one of the crew of the "Resolution" and of the "Discovery" during the third voyage of Captain Cook. <u>MS</u>, in <u>Provincial Library, Victoria</u> (typed copy). 465

GILBERT, Walter Edwin. <u>Arctic Pilot</u> (London, 1940). Life and work on North Canadian air routes; experiences recounted to Kathleen Shackleton. 466

GILKISON, Robert (d. 1845). Business journal, April-October, 1838; a shipbuilder's notes on shipping in connection with the 1837 rebellion. <u>MS, Public Archives, Toronto</u>; extracts in <u>Niagara Hist. Soc. Pubs. XVIII</u> (1909) 29-35. 467

GILKISON, Capt. William (b. 1777). Private diary, 1831-1832; travel in Scotland and England; farming at Grand River, Q., travel in Ontario; social conditions; cholera outbreak. <u>MS</u>, typewritten transcript, <u>Collection Gagnon</u>, Montreal Public Library. 468

GILL, E. A. W. <u>A Manitoba Chore Boy</u> (London, 1912). Experiences of a young English emigrant in Western Canada. 469

GILIHAM, Charles Edward. Raw North (New York, 1947). Travels and work of a conservationist in the far North; Eskimos and trappers; unglamorized picture. 470

GILLIS, James D. (b. 1870). A Little Sketch of My Life (Halifax, 1933?). Notes of a Canadian teacher; pedagogy; writer of textbooks; political views. Pamphlet; a copy at Harvard Library. 471

GILLMORE, Parker. Lone Life (London, 1875) 2 vols. An account of his year in the Canadian wilderness, near Orillia, Ont.; country life, conditions, sport, Indians. 472

GILMOUR, John. Religious journal, July 1853-January, 1864; a Canadian Baptist preacher's travel and work. MS, McMaster University, 132 pages (also his note-book and a letter-book for 1825). 473

GIROD, Amury (d. 1837, of Varennes). Political journal, November-December, 1837; political activities among the French in Quebec; translated. Canadian Pub. Archives Report, 1923 (Ottawa, 1924) 370-380. 474

GLADMAN, Henry (1834-1912). A fur-trader's journal, October 1857-June 1858; occupations around Fort William; factor of Hudson's Bay Company; visit to Red River. MS, Public Archives, Toronto, 57 pp. 475

GLEDHILL, Lieut. Col. Samuel. Memoirs, ed. W. H. Chippindall (Kendal, 1910). His work and private affairs while commander-in-chief of Newfoundland, 1709-1727. 476

GLENNIE, James H., of Baltimore. Travel diary, June-September 1800; from Maryland to Ontario and Quebec; tourist's notes; water-color sketches. MS, McGill University, D.25. 477

GODDEN, John. Notes and Reminiscences of a Journey to England (Montreal, 1873). Not seen; copy at Dennis College, Acadia University. 478

GODSELL, Philip Henry (born 1889). Red Hunters of the Snows (London, 1938). An account of thirty years experiences with Eskimos and Indians of Canadian Northwest and Arctic, while inspecting officer for Hudson's Bay Company; travels around Hudson's Bay, Saskatchewan, Athabasca; fur-trade and native life; good. The Vanishing Frontier (Toronto, 1939) covers similar material, as also does his Arctic Trader (Toronto, 1943). 479

GOFORTH, Mrs. Rosalind (Bell-Smith) (b.1864). Climbing (Grand Rapids, 1940). The memories of the wife of an evangelical missionary in Canada. 480

GOLDIE, John (1793-1886). Travel diary, 1819; a Canadian botanist's journey from Montreal to York, Lake Simcoe, Niagara, New York state; botanical notes. Diary of a Journey through Upper Canada (Toronto, 1897). 481

GOLDSMITH, Oliver (1787-1861). Autobiography, ed. W.E. Myatt (Toronto, 1943). Notes on the career of a Canadian poet in the government service; travels abroad. 482

GOMERY, Percy. "The Side Door to the Klondike," Canadian Bankers' Assoc.Jour. XXX (1923) passim. Reminiscences and personal experiences in the 1898 gold-rush; travel via Stikine River and Cassiar country. 483

GOODHAND, Henrietta McIntosh. Foot Prints (1948).Pioneer life in western Ontario from a woman's viewpoint;farming, domestic, religious life; covers 1880-1934. 484

GORDON, Captain. Military journal, April-August, 1758; siege of Louisbourg; activities of the artillery; mostly military details. Nova Scotia Hist. Society Colls. V (1886-1887) pp. 97-153. 485

GORDON, Rev. Daniel Miner (1845-1925). "Reminiscences of the North-West Rebellion Campaign of 1885," Queen's Quarterly, XI (1903) 3-20. A valuable account of his adventures in the Riel rebellion; military details of the campaign; a lively record. 486

GORDON, William Augustus. Military journal, April-August, 1758; account of his service with the Highland infantry in the siege of Louisbourg. Royal United Service Inst. Jour. LX (1915) 117-152. 487

GÖTSCH-TREVELYAN, Miss Katherine.Unharboured Heaths (Toronto, 1930). A young woman's experiences in Canada; Quebec; Ontario; Western Canada; personal reactions. 488

GOUGH, Lieut. Thomas Bunbury. Boyish Reminiscences (Toronto, 1910). Slight reminiscences of the King's visit to Canada, while he was a boy in Toronto. 489

GRACE, Henry. The History of the Life and Sufferings of Henry Grace (Reading, 1764). An Autobiography of British soldier captured by the French and Indians in Nova Scotia; account of his Indian captivity and ransom. 490

GRAHAM, Mrs. Emma (Jeffers) (d. 1922). "Three Years among the Ojibways, 1857-1860," Women's Canadian Hist. Soc. (1916-17) 35-40. Reminiscences by the daughter of a minister to the Ojibway Indians at Rice Lake, Ont. 491

GRAHAM, James Stevenson. A Scotch-Irish Canadian Yankee (New York, 1939). Autobiography of his life in Ontario, on the Canadian prairies, and later in the U.S.A. 492

GRANGE, Herbert. An English Farmer in Canada (London, 1904). Travels in Canada; farming notes and observations; police, law and general conditions; the records of a practical traveller. 493

GRANT, Mrs. Forsyth. "Bygone Days in Toronto," Canadian Mag. 1914, passim. Reminiscences of her social life fifty years before. 494

GRANT, George Monro (1835-1902). Ocean to Ocean (London, 1873) A diary of travel from the Atlantic to the Pacific in 1872; on the Sandford Fleming expedition through Canada; work as engineer of the Canadian Pacific Railway. 495

GRANT, John. Surveyor's journal, November 1863-February 1864; his work surveying the township of Assiginack on Manitoulin Island. MS, Toronto Public Libraries, 20 pp. 496

GRANT, Kenneth James. My Missionary Memories (Halifax, 1923). The experiences of a Canadian missionary to East Indians in Trinidad; his life in Nova Scotia in the early days of Queen Victoria. 497

GRANT, Sergeant Reginald. S. O. S. Stand to! (New York, 1918) Personal experiences of three years with the First Canadian Division in France during World War I; with the artillery at Ypres, Givenchy, Somme, and Vimy Ridge. 498

GRAVES, William, of New Ross, Scotland. Travel journal, May-September, 1820; via Quebec, Montreal, Great Lakes, Toronto, Niagara, and return; notes on topography; and social conditions. MS, McGill University, D.30 (typed copy). 499

GREEN, Rev. Anson (b. 1801). The Life and Times of the Reverend Anson Green (Toronto, 1877). Autobiography of a Methodist missionary in Canada; travels on Ontario circuits; organization of Methodist meetings in Toronto Area. 500

GREEN, Gavin Hamilton (born 1862, of Goderich). The Old Log-School (Goderich, Ont., 1939). Reminiscences of childhood and schooling in Ontario; country life among pioneer settlers from the 1860's. The Old Log House and Bygone Days in Our Village (Goderich, 1948). Reminiscences of school, town church, and social life in Goderich. 501

GRENFELL, Sir Wilfred Thomason (1865-1940). A Labrador Doctor (Boston, 1919). Autobiography of a missionary doctor; his medical training in London; his missionary and medical work among fisherman in Labrador and northern Newfoundland; Eskimos; wide travels during over thirty years. This was revised and brought up to date in; Forty Years for Labrador (New York, 1932). See also, "Life in Labrador," Blackwood's Mag., November, 1901, and, "Work among Labrador Fishermen," Canadian Club, Toronto, II (1904-1905), 156-161. 502

[GREY, Lieut. Col. Charles (1804-1870)]. Travel diary, June-August, 1839; from Montreal through Upper Canada, and from there to New York. MS, Toronto Public Libraries. 503

GREY, Lady Louise Elizabeth (died 1841). Social diary, April-December, 1838; public and social life of the family of the Governor-General; private and official. Lit. Hist.Society Quebec, 9th Ser. (1915) 7-61. 504

GREY OWL (George Stansfield Belaney, 1888-1938). Pilgrims of the Wild (Toronto, 1934).An autobiography of a writer, born in England, who lived as an Indian; covering years spent in northern Ontario and in the Temiscouata district of Quebec; beavers, conservation, writing. 505

GRIESBACH, Gen. William Antrobus (1878-1945). I Remember (Toronto, 1946). Reminiscences of family and private life; his military career; politics, public affairs, social life, and sports; largely in Edmonton. 506

GRIFFIN, Frederick. Variety Show (London, 1937). Reminiscences of a Canadian journalist; reporter on Toronto Star from 1916; Canada during World War I; visit of Prince of Wales; his work and chief experiences. 507

[GRIFFIN, Justus A.] Military diary, October-November 1871; a private soldier's account of the Red River expedition; his observations upon army conditions and travel, Indians, etc. From Toronto to Fort Garry (Hamilton, 1893); a pamphlet in Ottawa Archives. 508

GRIFFIN, Watson. The Gulf of Years (Toronto, 1927?). Contents
unknown. Since found to be fiction. 509

GRIFFITH, Arthur George Frederick (1838-1908). Fifty Years
of Public Service (London, 1904). Includes a section on his
military service in Canada. 510

GRIGNON, Edmond (born 1861). En Guettant les Ours (Montreal,
1931). Happy memories of medical life and labors; a country
physician in the Laurentians. Quarante Ans sur le Bout du
Banc (Montreal, 1932). Reminiscences of his work as a justice of the Peace. 511

GROUARD, Mgr. (b. 1840, Vicar of Athabasca). Souvenirs de Ma
Soixante Ans d'Apostolat (Winnipeg, n.d.). His training as
a missionary; missionary labors and travels in the Canadian
Northwest, 1862-1920; the Mackenzie River, Yukon, Klondyke,
Athabasca; travels in Europe; Indians, Eskimos; incidental
general matters. 512

GROVE, Frederick Philip (1872-1948). In Search of Myself (Toronto, 1946). Autobiography of a Canadian author; childhood
in Sweden; education in Europe; emigration and experiences
in Canada. 513

GUNN, Marcus (b. 1798? of London, Ont.). Private diary, January 1830-December 1854; his emigration to Canada as a boy;
reading, religion, weather, family life;travels in Ontario;
theological studies and work as publisher of the Universal-
ist Advocate and religious tracts and papers; universalism,
temperance movement, spiritualism, etc;a huge and interesting document. Typed copy, Ottawa Archives, from a MS owned
in 1938 by Miss Nellie Gunn, of London, Ont. 514

GUNN, Peter. Fur-trader's journal, 1886-1893; work and trade
at Fort St. John. MS, Alberta Prov. Library. Edmonton. 515

GUPPY, Bill (b. 1875). Bill Guppy, King of the Woodsmen.(London, 1940). Autobiography recorded by Hal Pink; hunting and
trapping in Northern Ontario; meetings with Grey Owl. 516

HADFIELD, Joseph (1759-1851). Travel journal, June to October,
1785; a Manchester man's tour from New York to Montreal and
Quebec; meetings with distinguished persons. An Englishman
in America, ed. D. S. Robertson (Toronto, 1933). 517

[HAGERMAN, Lieut.Col. Christopher Alexander (1792-1847)]. War
journal,November 1813-June 1814; military events of the war
described by Drummond's aide-de-camp. MS,Toronto Public Libraries. 518

HAIG-THOMAS, David. *I Leap before I Look* (London, 1936). Includes a section on sports and climbing in Canada. 519

HAIGHT, Canniff (1825-1901). *Country Life in Canada Fifty Years Ago* (Toronto, 1885). Pioneering life in Upper Canada; schools, institutions, social events, farming, work; family and personal affairs. See also his "Canadian Life in the Country Fifty Years Ago," *Canadian Monthly*, IV (1880); and "Ontario, Fifty Years Ago and Now," *Canadian Monthly*, Volume VI (1881) 443-454, 556-577. 520

HALDIMAND, General Sir Frederick (1718-1791). Private diary January 1786-August 1790; social and political life in Canada; gossipy and intimate. *Report Canadian Archives, 1889* (Ottawa, 1890) 124-299. 521

HALL, Charles. Travel Journal, December 1861-February 1862; a journey with the Prince Consort's Own Rifle Brigade, from Ireland to Hamilton, Upper Canada. *Typed copy*, Toronto Public Library, 22 pp. 522

HALL, Charles Frances (1821-1871). *Life with the Esquimaux* (London, 1864). Search in a whaling barque, 1860-1862, for survivors of Sir John Franklin's expedition; Frobisher Bay region; Eskimo life. 523

HALL, Mrs. Mary Georgina Caroline. *A Lady's Life on a Farm in Manitoba* (London, 1884). A journal of farm-life, 1882; based upon letters. 524

HALLIDAY, William May (b. 1866). *Potlatch and Totem* (London, 1935). His labors as a student of Indian customs in British Columbia; recollections of life and work as an Indian Agent for thirty-eight years. 525

HAM, George Henry (1847-1926). *Reminiscences of a Raconteur* (Toronto, 1921). A Canadian journalist's reminiscences and anecdotes of politics, public affairs, celebrities, pioneer life, in Toronto, Winnipeg, and Montreal. 526.

HAMILTON, Lord Frederic. *Here, There, and Everywhere* (London 1921). His travel and diplomatic life, including experiences in Canada. 527

HAMILTON, Captain Sir J. Military journal, December 1775-May 1776; good military details of the siege of Quebec. *A Journal of the Principal Occurrences during the Siege of Quebec*

(London, 1824); F. C. Würtele, Blockade of Quebec in 1775-1776 (Quebec, 1906). 528

HAMILTON, James H. (b.1879). Western Shores (Vancouver 1932). A personal narrative of maritime life on the coast of British Columbia. 529

HAMILTON, William Edwin (b. 1834). Peeps at My Life (Chatham, Ont., 1895). A brief autobiography of an Irishman who emigrated to Canada; facts about Chatham. Copy of this edition in Toronto Public Libraries. 530

HANBURY, David T. Sport and Travel in the Northland of Canada (London, 1904). Travels, 1898-1902, in Northwestern Canada, between Hudson's Bay and Mackenzie River; Indian and Eskimo customs. 531

HANGO, Angeline (b. 1909). Truthfully Yours (Toronto, 1948). Amusing story of French-Canadian family, told by the daughter; rural life, convent schools, old customs near Lake St. John, Quebec. 532

HANINGTON, Charles F. Travel journal, 1874-1875; an account of a winter journey from Quesnelle through the Rocky Mountains. Canadian Archives Report (1888) cx-cxxxii. 533

HANNA, David Blyth (1858-1938). Trains of Recollection (Toronto, 1924). His reminiscences of pioneer railroading in the Canadian west by an old railroad man; settlers; Indians and their ways. 534

HARDY, Capt. Campbell (1831-1919). Sporting Adventures in the New World (London, 1855) 2 vols. Experiences of a moose hunter in Nova Scotia and New Brunswick in the 1850's. 535

HARGRAVE, James (1798-1865). A fur-trader's journal, August 1828-May 1829; kept at York Factory; work with the Hudson's Bay Company; informal record. MS, McGill University, D.32; typed copy at Toronto Public Libraries. 536

HARMON, Daniel Williams (1778-1845). Fur-trader's diary, April 1800-August 1819; voyages from Montreal to the Pacific; the life of a trader in Athabasca and the Rockies: a partner in the Northwest Company. A Journal of Voyages and Travels in the Interior of North America (Andover, 1820). 537

HARRIS, Mrs. Amelia, of London, Ont. Private diary, 1857-1877; notes on society and domestic life in London; local events, rumors, visits of celebrities. Extracts published by Professor Fred Landon in London Free Press, July-November 1928; clippings in University of Toronto Library. 538

HARRIS, Charlotte (d. 1854, of London, Ont.). Private diary, October 1848-January 1851; a pleasant record of social and domestic life in London; amusements and visits. Selections published by Professor Fred Landon in the London Free Press beginning September 19, 1928; cuttings in University of Toronto Library. 539

HARRIS, Odee. Unsettled in Places (London, 1937). Including a section on travel and journalistic work in Canada. 540

HARRISON, Alfred H. In Search of a Polar Continent (Toronto, 1908). An exploration journey, 1905-1907, by the Mackenzie route to the Arctic Ocean; explorations of Mackenzie delta; Eskimos, Arctic travel. 541

HARROLD, E. W. The Diary of Our Own Pepys (Toronto, 1947). A selection from his column in the Ottawa Citizen, 1930-1945; journalistic notes on personal, public, and domestic trivia in Canada; imitation of Pepys. 542

HART-McHARG, W. From Quebec to Pretoria (Toronto, 1902). His narrative of his personal experiences during service in the Boer War in South Africa; with Canadian forces. 543

HARTNEY, Harold Evans (born 1888). Up and at 'Em (Harrisburg, Pa., 1940). Experiences of a Canadian in World War I, with the Royal Flying Corps, and later as commander of the First Pursuit Group of U.S. Air Service. 544

HARTWELL, George E. Granary of Heaven (Toronto, 1939). Record of religious life; not seen. 545

HASKELL, W. B. Two Years in the Klondike (Hartford, 1898). A good narrative of the gold-rush by a returned miner; conditions in Dawson; Canadian Mounted Police. 546

HASWELL, Robert. Exploration journal, September 1787 to June 1789; voyage around the world on the Columbia-Rediviva and the sloop Washington. Typed copy in the Provincial Library, Victoria; consult also, Hubert H. Bancroft, History of the Northwest Coast, Vol. I, passim. Exploration journal, September 1790-October 1791; the log of the second voyage of the Columbia; exploration on Northwest coast. Photostat of

MS, Washington University Library. His exploration journal, August 1791-May 1793; discovery and explorations on the Columbia-Rediviva. Transcript in Library Association of Portland and University of Washington Library; extracts in Bancroft, op. cit. 547

HATHAWAY, Ann (b. 1849, of Muskoka). Muskoka Memories (Toronto, 1904). Reminiscences of pioneer farming near Toronto in the seventies and later; social, domestic, and family. 548

HATHAWAY, S. G. Mining diary, 1862; notes kept by an American miner in the Cariboo,.B.C. Canadian Hist. Rev. XIII (1932) 291-299. 549

HAVENS, William V. (1829-1910). Private diary, January-December, 1872; life and work on a farm at Aldborough, Ont. MS, Toronto Public Libraries, 81 pp. (typed copy). 550

HAWEIS, Rev. H. R. Travel and Talk (London, 1896). Including a record of his religious work and travel in Canada. 551

HAYNE, M. H. E. Pioneers of the Klondike (London, 1897). An autobiography of his two years' police service in the Yukon during the gold-rush; recorded by H. W. Taylor. 552

HEAD, Sir Francis Bond (1793-1875).A Narrative (London 1839); The Emigrant (London, n.d.). His experiences of political and military life in Canada, including a brief spell as the Governor-General in Upper Canada in 1835;emigrants and settlers; the 1837 rebellion. 553

HEAD, Sir George (1782-1855). Forest Scenes and Incidents in the Wilds of North America (London, 1829). A winter journey from Halifax to Lake Simcoe, and residence there. 554

HEALY, William Joseph (b. 1867). Women of Red River (Winnipeg 1923). Based on the recollections of women settlers of the early days of the Red River settlement. 555

HEARNE, Samuel (1745-1792). Travel diary, November 1769-June 1772; three trips by land northwest from Hudson's Bay; natural history; Indians.A Journey from Prince of Wales's Fort in Hudson's Bay to the Northern Ocean (London,1795;Toronto, 1911). Travel diary, June 1774-October 1775; through northern Canada, west of Hudson's Bay. Journals of Samuel Hearne and Philip Turnor, ed. J. B. Tyrrell (Toronto, 1934) pp.95-194. 556

HELMCKEN, John Sebastian (1823-1920). A reminiscence of 1850; gives description of Fort Victoria; physician with Hudson's Bay Company. MS, Provincial Library, Victoria (typewritten copy). 557

HEMSLEY, Richard (b. 1846). Looking Back (Montreal, 1930). A watchmaker and jeweller in Montreal, 1867-1890; accounts of his business, the town, and travels abroad. 558

HENDERSON, Mrs.Mary Le Rossignol (Gillespie) (1840-1935). Memories of My Early Years (Montreal, 1937). Autobiography of her early life in the province of Quebec. 559

HENDERSON, Mrs. Millicent Pollock (Steele), and MURRAY, Ellen Frances (Steele). Travel journal, April-August, 1833; from England to Simcoe County, U.C., thro' New York; social life on shipboard; clearing site for farm, homemaking, social affairs, amusements; a lively record. Ontario Hist. Society Papers and Recs. XXIII (1926) 483-510. 560

HENRY, Alexander (1739-1824). Travels and Adventures in Canada ed. James Bain (Toronto, 1901). Exploration and travels in the fur-trade, 1760-1766, from Montreal to Athabasca;one of standard sources on the history of the fur trade in Canada, and on travel conditions, social life, etc. 561

HENRY, Alexander (d. 1814). Travel and fur-trading journals, July 1800-May 1814; explorations and fur-trade in the Great Northwest; work at posts in Saskatchewan, Astoria, Columbia River area, on behalf of Northwest Company; minute details; nephew of the foregoing. In Elliott Coues, New Light on the Early History of the Greater Northwest (New York, 1897), 3 vols. 562

HENRY, Anthony. Fur-trader's journal, June 1754-June 1755;at York Factory, Hudson's Bay Company; a journey to country of the Blackfeet Indians; topography, Indians, trade, rivalry of French. Proc. and Trans. Royal Society Canada, 3d Ser. I (1907) Sec. II, 307-354. 563

HENRY, George, of Galt, Ontario "Reminiscences of a Pioneer," MS,University of Toronto Library, 32 pp. (typewritten copy). His experience in Canada, 1878-1910; excursion to Manitoba to survey for a settlement; wheat farming in the Red River country; the Riel rebellion. 564

HENRY, Walter. Trifles from My Portfolio (Quebec, 1839), two vols. Experiences during twenty-nine years as an army surgeon in Canada. 565

HENSON, Rev. Josiah. Father Henson's Story (Boston, 1858). An American negro slave and Methodist; includes his life as an exile in Canada, and life of negroes there. 566

HERRING, Mrs. Frances Elizabeth (Clarke) (born 1851). Canadian Camp Life (London, 1900); Among the People of British Columbia (London, 1903); In the Pathless West (London, 1904). Her domestic life in Victoria; reminiscences of soldiers, pioneers, Indians, in British Columbia. 567

HERVEY, William (1732-1815). Military journal, June 1755-December 1814; includes military service in British America from 1755-1763, and service at Montreal; additions by other writers. Journals of the Hon. William Hervey in North America and Europe (Bury St. Edmonds, 1906). 568

HIGINBOTHAM, John David (born 1864). When the West Was Young (Toronto, 1933). An autobiography of life in Ontario and as pioneer farmer in the Canadian West from 1884. 569

HILL, Alexander Staveley. From Home to Home (New York, 1885). A personal narrative of an Englishman's summer holidays, in the Canadian northwest, 1881 to 1884. 570

HILL, Allan Massie (1876-1943). It Happened to Me (Toronto, 1942). Incidents in a minister's life in Nova Scotia. 571

HILTS, Joseph Henry (1819-1903). Experiences of a Backwoods Preacher (Toronto, 1892). Thirty years' work as a Methodist minister on the Ontario circuits; travels, ministry, medical work, frontier life and conditions. 572

HINCKS, Sir Francis (1807-1885). Reminiscences of Public Life (Montreal, 1884). Political affairs in Upper Canada, 1836-1855; the 1836 rebellion; later Governor of British Guiana and the Windward Isles. 573

HINDS, E.M. Nothing Venture (London, 1940). An English schoolmistress; includes two years of life and work among French-Canadians near Regina. 574

HINES, John (b.1850). Red Indians of the Plains (London, 1915). An autobiography of his thirty years of travel and missionary labors in Saskatchewan. 575

HODGSON, F. T. "Reminiscences, 1848-1857," Papers and Records of Huron Inst. II (1914) pp. 3-12. Reminiscences of pioneers and pioneering; and of settlement of Collingwood district, Ontario. 576

HOLLIDAY, Charles William (born 1870). The Valley of Youth (Caldwell, Idaho, 1948). Reminiscences, chiefly of life in the Okanagan, B. C., fifty years before.   577

HOLT, C. E. An Autobiographical Sketch of a Teacher's Life (Quebec, 1875), with Supplement (Quebec, 1875). Childhood in Quebec; teaching in northern and southern states, California, Cuba, Peru; financial troubles in Quebec.   578

HOOKER, J. M. The Heart of an Immigrant (London, 1931). Personal record of his experiences in Canada.   579

HOPKIRK, James. Travel diary, 1835; experiences crossing the Atlantic, from Glasgow to New York; then to Hamilton, Ont.; his service with the government. Queen's Quar. XLII (1935) 55-67 (account and quotations).   580

HORNBY, John. Snow Man, by Malcolm Waldron (Boston, 1931) is a biography based on Hornby's journals; life and travels in the Far North of Canada, beyond Great Slave Lake; adventurous life in the twenties.   581

HOUGHTON, Frank. "A Reminiscence of a Sojourn at a Hudson Bay Post," Rod and Gun XIV (July, 1912) 145-158. Experiences at a post on Georgian Bay about 1887; Indian life; sport.   582

HOWARD, Mrs. Hilda (Williams) (b. 1887). The Glamour of British Columbia, by "H.Glynn-Ward" (Toronto, 1926). Her life in the West; on sea-coast; Rocky Mountains; hunting, trapping. Indians, places; rather impersonal.   583

HOWARD, John George (1803-1890). Incidents in the Life of John G. Howard, Esq. (Toronto, 1885). A short autobiography, based on diaries, of the man who gave High Park to the city of Toronto; emigration from England; his work in Canada as an architect and surveyor.   584

[HOWARD, Jonathan E. (born 1819)]. Life's Real Romance (Salt Lake City, 1883?). An Irish boy emigrant in Ontario in the sixties; farming there and life of early settlers. Copy at Harvard.   585

HOWARD, Lady Winifred. Journal of a Tour (London, 1897). Her notes during a tour; through United States, Canada, Mexico; Quebec, Montreal, Ottawa, Toronto, Niagara.   586

HOWE, Joseph (1804-1873, of Halifax). Political diary, 1861; his political activities, speeches, and travels while Prime

Minister of Nova Scotia. Travel diary, 1863; a trip to New Brunswick and the U.S.A.in connection with the Fishery Commission; topographical notes. MS, Howe Papers, Ottawa Archives. 587

HOWES, Ernest Albert (b. 1872). With a Glance Backward (Toronto, 1939). Farming life in western Ontario at the turn of the century; schools, churches, books, politics. 588

HOWEY, Florence R. (1856?-1936). Pioneering on the C. P. R. (Ottawa, 1938). Autobiography of the wife of a medical officer with the Canadian Pacific Railway in Ontario. 589

HOWISON, J. Sketches of Upper Canada (Edinburgh, 1821). Notes on pioneers and domestic life in Ontario; farming and other details for emigrants. 590

HUARD, Victor Alphonse (1853-1929). Labrador et Anticosti (Montreal, 1897). Travels in Labrador by a French-Canadian priest and author; Canadian and Acadian fishermen, Indians, etc. Impressions d'un Passant (Quebec, 1906). Travels in America, Europe and Africa, partly in diary form. 591

HUBBARD, Leonidas (1872-1939). Travel journal; kept during an expedition into Labrador; an exploration of river Nascaupee and River George. Mina E. H. Ellis, A Woman's Way through Unknown Labrador (New York, 1908), 205-254. 592

HUESTIS, Captain Daniel H. Adventures during His Banishment (Boston, 1848). Account of the 1837 rebellion and his part in it;captivity and political exile in Tasmania; of his experiences and hardships; release and journey home via California and U.S.A.: French-Canadian. A copy at Queen's University Library. 593

HUGHES, Thomas (1759-1790). Private diary, 1778-1789; an English volunteer's experience under Burgoyne during the American revolution; service in Quebec and Detroit; later social life and amusements in Quebec.A Journal, ed. E. A. Benians (London, 1947). 594

HULTON, Henry. Travel diary, 1772; a bitter account of Canada and its institutions by a Bostonian. Anne Hulton, Letters of a Loyalist Lady (Cambridge, 1927), 100-107. 595

HUNTER, Charles. "Reminiscences of the Fenian Raid, 1866," Niagara Hist. Soc. XX (1911), 1-22. His service as a young lad with the Barrie Rifles. 596

HUNTER, Martin (b. 1757). Private diary, 1808-1811 (extracts) notes on New Brunswick, where he was an administrator; social life in Fredericton. MS, Bailey Coll., in University

of New Brunswick.   Original MS owned by the Hunter family,
Anton's Hill, Berwickshire, Scotland.   597

HUTCHISON, Percy. Masquerade (London, 1936).An actor's reminiscences; includes an account of theatrical tours in Canada.   598

HUTTON, George A. (born 1830).   Reminiscences in the Life of George A.Hutton (London, 1907). A sergeant-major's autobiography; includes his service in Canada.   599

HUTTON, Dr. Samuel King (b. 1877).   Among the Eskimos of Labrador (London, 1912).   Five years of medical work among the Eskimos; native life and customs; hunting.   By Eskimo Dog-Sled and Kayak (London, 1918). Further experiences and travels of a medical missionary in Labrador.   600

HYATT, Capt. Ernest. All over the Place (London, 1936). Various travels and jobs; including service in Canadian Mounted Police, tracking Eskimo murderers in the Far North.   601

INGLIS, Right Rev.Charles (1734-1816, 1st Bishop of Nova Scotia).   Diaries and correspondence, 1775-1814; his diocesan work while Bishop of Nova Scotia; preaching, travel,organization, church work, journeys to England. Canadian Archives Report (1912), 215-288, and (1913), 227-283. Transcript of MS, Public Archives, Ottawa.   602

INGLIS, Right Rev. John (1777-1850, third Bishop of Nova Scotia).   Religious journal, 1843; visitation journeys in Nova Scotia, Cape Breton, and the eastern shore of New Brunswick. Church in the Colonies (London, 1846) 72 pp. Other diaries and correspondence were published in the Canadian Archives Report for 1912 and 1913; transcript of MS Public Archives, Ottawa.   603

INGSTAD, Helge Marcus (b. 1899). The Land of Feast and Famine (New York, 1933).   Autobiography of fishing and hunting in northwest Canada; translated from Norwegian.   604

IRWIN, David. One Man Against the North (London, 1940).   Lone hand in the Canadian Arctic, 1933-1934; solitary wanderings à la Rasmussen; living with Eskimos off the land; a barely told record of remarkable adventures and hardships.   605

IRWIN, John (1826-1907). Travel diary, April-September 1841; from England to London, Ontario, and life there. MS, Lawson Memorial Library, University of Western Ontario, 16 pp. and Toronto Public Libraries.   606

IRWIN, Ruth (Inglis). Retaliation (Victoria, 1923). Autobiography of childhood and her later troubled period in mental institutions, suffering from a persecution complex. A copy in Bibliothèque St. Sulpice. 607

ANON. Items in the Life of an Usher (Montreal, 1850). A copy in the Ontario Education Department Library Toronto. See No. 1160. 608

JACKSON, John Richard (1787-1847, of Montreal). Religious diary, July 1807-September 1808; details of his conversion to Catholicism; mysticism; travel notes. U. S. Catholic Hist. Mag. I (1887) 92-100. 609

JACKSON, Mary Percy. On the Last Frontier (London, 1933). Her experiences of pioneer farming; Peace River block. 610

JACOBS, Rev. Peter. Travel diary, May-August 1852; the journey of an Ojibway Indian Methodist minister from Rice Lake to Hudson's Bay and return; his work and hardships. Journal of the Rev. Peter Jacobs (Toronto, 1853). 611

JAMES, Norman B. Autobiography of a Nobody (Toronto, 1947). Experiences of cattle ranching and cow-punching in Calgary, 1893; work as a Social Creditor in Alberta. 612

JAMES, Thomas (1593?-1635?). Exploration journal, May 1631-October 1632; a search for the Northwest Passage; James and Hudson's Bay; a day to day account. The Dangerous Voyage of Capt. Thomas James (London, 1633). 613

JAMIESON, John? Private diary, April-June 1854; life on farm in Adelaide Township, Upper Canada; weather, local politics, church. MS, Toronto Public Libraries, 50 pp. (a typewritten copy). 614

JARRET , Andrée (i.e., Cécile Beauregard). Moisson de Souvenirs (Montreal, 1919). Memories of her childhood, holidays, convent schooling, her religious life among French Canadian family. A copy in Collection Gagnon, Montreal Public Library. 615

JARVIS, P. R. (1824-1906, of Toronto). Memoirs of P.R. Jarvis (n.p., n.d.). Autobiography and diary; early life in Ontario; travels to New Orleans and China; good personal detail of a sailor's life. 616

JARVIS, Colonel Stephen. "Reminiscences of a Loyalist," Canadian Mag. XXVI (January-April, 1906). His experience after the American Revolution; English soldier in Canada. 617

JARVIS, Colonel Weston (born 1857). Jottings from an Active Life (London, 1928). An autobiography of a military career; includes a section on his service in Canada. 618

JEFFERSON, Robert. "Fifty Years on the Saskatchewan," Canadian North-West Hist. Soc. Pubs. I, No.5 (1929) 160 pp. Autobiography of English boy, who went to the Canadian West, in 1878; life as a teacher among the Indians; Indian customs; Rebellion of 1885. 619

JENKINSON, Sir Anthony Banks (b. 1912). Where Seldom a Gun is Heard (London, 1937). His travel, social life, and sport in Canada in the thirties; lively comments on towns and people from coast to coast. 620

JÉRÉMIE, Nicolas (1669-1732).Twenty Years of York Factory,ed. R. Douglas and J. N. Wallace (Ottawa, 1926). Services with the Hudson's Bay Company, 1694-1714; at Strait and Bay; his travels and work in the fur trade; translated from a French edition of 1720. 621

JEWITT, John Rodgers (1783-1821). The Adventures of John Jewitt (London, 1896). The famous narrative of his three years as a captive of the Nootka Indians on Vancouver Island;very good description of Indian life. 622

JOHNSON, Rev. F. "Reminiscences of Fifty Years in the Methodist Church"; brief reminiscences of travels and ministry on Ontario circuits. MS, Victoria College, Toronto, Archives Dept., Pam. T. 123, Joh., 12 pp. 623

JOHNSON, John (b. 1860). Childhood, Travel, and British Columbia (Abertillery, Mon., 1907). Autobiography; a Norwegian childhood, life as a sailor, and his experiences in British Columbia. 624

JOHNSON, Richard Byron. Very Far West Indeed (London, 1872). The disenchanted narrative of travel and experiences of an emigrant in British Columbia and the Pacific Northwest; the frontier life; mining, rustling, adventures. 625

JOLLIET, Louis (died 1694). Exploring journals, May-August, 1694; explorations of Labrador and its coast; natural history and topography; in French. Rapport de l'Archiviste de ...Québec, pour 1943-1944 (Quebec, 1944) 147-206. 626

JONES, C. J. Buffalo Jones: Forty Years of Adventure, compiled by Colonel Henry Inman (London, 1899). A Kansas man's narrative of his experience with bison and musk-oxen in the Canadian North, Hudson's Bay, Manitoba; adventures, travels, hunting; apparently based on a diary. 627

JONES, Henry John. Settler's diary, 1833-1839 (extracts); the experiences and work of an early settler and farmer, in Ontario and Upper Canada. Willison's Monthly, IV (April-September) passim. 628

JONES, Rev. Peter (1802-1856). Autobiography and diary, 1802-1838; travel and ministry of native Indian missionary known as Kah-ke-wa-quo-nā-by; Methodist labours among Mohawks and Ojibways in Ontario; good and detailed picture of Christian morality and Indian customs, and his early work and schooling. Life and Journals (Toronto, 1860). 629

JUKES, Joseph Beete. Excursions in and about Newfoundland (London, 1842) two vols. A geological survey, with descriptions of towns, peoples, social life, customs, general conditions, pests, and inconveniences. Copy at McGill University Library. 630

KAIN, Conrad (1858-1934). Where the Clouds Can Go (New York, 1935). Autobiography of Austrian mountain guide; from 1909 in British Columbia; farming, hunting, climbing. 631

KALM, Pehr (1716-1779). Travel journals, August 1748-October 1749; the last four months dealing with travel, people, and natural history in Canada; from Montreal to the Montmorency River. Travels into North America (London, 1770-1771) three vols. 632

KANE, Paul (1810-1871, of York). Painter's diary, May 1846-October 1848; travels of a painter among the Indians; from Toronto to Vancouver and back; adventures, Indian life and character. Wanderings of an Artist (London, 1859); ed. L.J. Burpee (Toronto, 1925).Others of his writings dealing with his life and travels among Indian tribes in western Canada are: Incidents of Travel on the North-West Coast (London, 1855); Notes of a Sojourn among the Half-Breeds (London, 1856; Notes of Travel among the Walla-Walla Indians (London 1856); The Chinook Indians (London, 1857). 633

KEAN, Captain Abram (born 1855, of Flowers Island). Old and Young Ahead (London, 1935). Autobiography of a seal-hunter from 1855 to 1934; life in Labrador and Newfoundland; ice-hunting and seal-fishing; cod and herring fishing in Newfoundland; economic problems; cabinet minister in Newfoundland. 634

KELLEY, Right Rev. Francis Clement (b. 1870). The Bishop Jots It Down (New York,1939). Autobiography of a Roman Catholic bishop; first part deals with his early life in Prince Edward Island; later work in U.S.A. 635

KELSEY, Henry (1670?-1724?). Fur-trader's journal, June 1689-August 1721; travels and trading with Hudson's Bay Company; exploration, Indian life; York Fort. The Kelsey Papers, ed. A. G. Doughty and C. Martin (Ottawa, 1929). 636

KENDALL, Captain H. G. (b. 1874). Adventures on the High Seas (London, 1939). Includes details of his service on Canadian Pacific liners. 637

KENNEDY, David. Kennedy's Colonial Travel (London, 1876). The record of a peregrinating Scot; partly in Canada. 638

KENNEDY, David (1825-1886, of Guelph). Incidents in Pioneer Days (Toronto, 1903). His farming on the St. Lawrence from 1829; a simple account of social, family, religious affairs and adventures. 639

KENNEDY, Howard Angus."Memories of '85," Canadian Geog. Jour. XI (1935) 55-64. His experiences as a war-correspondent in the campaigns of Canadian troops against Métis and Indians; 1885 rebellion. 640

KENNEDY, Sir William Robert (1838-1916). Sports, Travel, and Adventure in Newfoundland (Edinburgh, 1885). Reminiscences of sailor's life; at Newfoundland and West Indians stations from 1879 to 1883; trade, sport, social, customs. 641

KERR, Wilfred Brenton (b. 1896). Shrieks and Crashes (Toronto, 1929). Personal narrative of his service with Canadian troops in France during 1st World War; 1917. 642

KEYSERLINGK, Robert Wendelin. Unfinished History (London, 1948). Autobiography; his Russian childhood; experiences in Russian revolution and Hitler's Germany; settlement in Quebec Province; politics and war. 643

KING, Amabel. Relics of a V. A. D. (Toronto, 1935). Contents unknown. 644

KING, Dr. Richard (1811?-1876). Narrative of a Journey to the Shores of the Arctic Ocean (London, 1836) two vols. Experiences of the surgeon-naturalist on expedition under command of Captain Back in 1833-1835; through Canada to the shores of the Arctic; Eskimos, Indians, natural history. 645

KINGSTON, William H. G. Western Wanderings (London, 1856) two vols. A detailed account of holiday in Quebec and Ontario; principal towns; politics; visits to literary men. 646

KINTON, Ada Florence (1859-1905). Just One Blue Bonnet, ed. by Sara A. Randleson (Toronto, 1907). Extracts from the diary and letters of an English girl who came to Muskoka, Ontario, and worked with the Salvation Army. 647

KIRBY, William. Diaries and notebooks of this Canadian author (no dates given). MS, Lorne Pierce Collection, Queen's University, Kingston, Ont. 648

KIRK, Robert C. Twelve Months in Klondike (London, 1897). The record of an early arrival, 1897; some early details of the gold-rush; useful. 649

KIRKPATRICK, George Bromly (1835-1917). Work diary, 1874; his occupation as a surveyor in the Crown Lands Department, Toronto. MS, Public Archives, Toronto, 104 pp. 650

KLENGENBERG, Christian (1869-1931). Klengenberg of the Arctic, ed. Tom MacInnis (London, 1932). Autobiography of a Danish born Arctic sailor, trader, traveller, who became an American and later a Canadian citizen; the Canadian Arctic. 651

KNIGHT, E. Lorne, of Vancouver. Arctic diary, September 1921-March 1923; with Stefansson's Arctic expedition; voyage to Wrangel Island. Photostat of MS, University of Toronto Library. 652

KNIGHT, George Wilson (b. 1897, of Toronto). Atlantic Crossing (London, 1936). The Canadian professor's artistic and emotional experiences; Canada and England. 653

KNIGHT, Capt. James. (d. 1720?). Fur-trader's journal, July-September 1717; from York Fort to Churchill River to found a Hudson's Bay Company fort; travel dangers and adventures. James F. Kenney, The Founding of Churchill (Toronto, 1932), 111-189. 654

KNOX, Capt. John (d. 1778). Military journal, February 1757-September 1760; very detailed and valuable account of campaigns during the French and Indian War; Louisbourg and Quebec, etc. An Historical Journal of the Campaigns in North-America (London, 1769); ed. A. G. Doughty (Toronto, 1914, 2 vols. 655

KOHLMEISTER, Benjamin Gottlieb (1785?-1874) and KNOCH, George (1770?-1857). Religious journal, June-October, 1811; journey of Moravian (Unitas Fratrum) missionaries to Ungava Bay to explore the coast and convert the Eskimos. Journal of a Voyage from Okkak on the Coast of Labrador to Ungava Bay (London, 1814). 656

LABADIE, Louis Génereux, of Quebec. Teacher's journal, 1794-1815; charming and delicate notes on his work as a teacher, his friends and pupils, at Vercheres; celebrations, feasts, domestic life; poems; French. MS, Archives of Séminaire de Québec; typewritten copy in Ottawa Archives. 657

LACASSE, Z. Une Mine de Souvenirs (Quebec, 1920). A Catholic priest's memories of his childhood and family in the 1850's schooling, religious training, and missionary work in Saskatchewan; politics and religion; pleasant sketches. 658

LACROIS, Émilie (Fortin) Tremblay (b. 1872). Une Pionnière du Yukon (Chicoutimi, Que., 1948). Reminiscences of the first white woman to cross the Chilcoot Pass; life in the Klondike; ed. by M. Bobillier. 659

LAMBERT, Adélard (born 1867). Journal d'un Bibliophile (Drummondville, Que., 1927). Experiences of a collector of books and autographs; sales, collections, books; copy at Bibliothèque St. Sulpice. 660

LAND, John (b. 1806). "Recollections," Wentworth Hist. Society Papers, VIII (1919) 20-24. The personal reminiscences of a militia man's resistance against the rebels in 1837. 661

LANDERY, Charles. So What? (London, 1938). A young man's travels and adventures; including a section on his experiences in Canada. 662

LANDMANN, Colonel (born 1780). Adventures and Recollections (London, 1852) 2 vols. Includes his experiences in Canada, 1797-1805; social affairs, customs, personalities in Quebec and Montreal. 663

LANE, William H. Private diary, February 1865-July 1867; his work as a farmer and notes on weather, crops, etc. MS, Public Archives, Toronto, 112 pages. Private diary, 1886-1889, notes on his work as farmer and lighthouse-keeper at False Ducks. MS, Public Archives, Toronto, 61 pp. 664

LANGSLOW, Richard. Travel diary, September-October 1817; from Connecticut to Niagara Falls; to Queenston, and Fort Erie;a captain in the East India Company. MS, Toronto Public Libraries, 27 pp. (typewritten copy). 665

LANGTON, Anne (d. 1893). The Story of Our Family (Manchester, 1881). Mainly an autobiography; life in England and Europe; settlement in Sturgeon Lake district, Ontario. 666

LAPOINTE, Arthur Joseph (b. 1895). War diary, September 1916-February 1919; experiences of a Quebec soldier with the Canadians in France. Soldier of Quebec (Montreal, 1931). 667

LA ROCHEFOUCAULT LIANCOURT, Francois Alexandre Frédéric. Voyage dans les États-Unis d'Amèrique (Paris, 1799), 8 volumes trans. Henry Newman (1799). The third volume deals with his travels and observations in Canada,1795; the fortifications and soldiers; Governor Simcoe; general conditions, culture, farming; an interesting survey. 668

LAROCQUE, François Antoine, of Montreal. Fur-trader's diary, June to October, 1805; from Fort de la Bosse to Yellowstone trade and trapping for Hudson's Bay Company; Crow Indians, topography, adventures. Canadian Archives Pubs. (1910) No. 3, 82 pp. Translated in Frontier and Midland (Montana) XIV and XV (1933-1935),reprinted as Sources of Northwest History No. 20. 669

LARTIQUE, Mgr. Religious journal, 1819; work in the Montreal diocese. MS, Ottawa Archives, Archévêché de Montréal, Carton 9, Pt. 2. 670

LATERRIÈRE, Pierre de Sales (b. 1747). Mémoires (Quebec 1873) Early adventures de coeur in France, a journey to New World medical studies at Harvard;removal to Quebec; his marriage, family complications, domestic affairs. 671

LAURE, Rev.Pierre Michel (1688-1738). Relation Inédite, 1720 à 1730 (Montreal,1889). The record of a Jesuit's mission to the Saguenay. Copy in Bibliothèque St. Sulpice. 672

LAURISTON, Victor (b. 1881). Inglorious Milton (Chatham, Ont. 1934). Autobiography of a Canadian story writer, mixture of fiction, history, autobiography. 673

LA VALLÉE, Jeannine, of Montreal. Mea Culpa (Montreal, 1934). Childhood and education in Canada;his experience in France;

return to Canada; French Canadian patriotism. Copy in Collection Gagnon, Montreal Public Library. 674

LAVERGNE, Armand, of Quebec. Trente Ans de Vie Nationale (Montreal, 1934). French-Canadian life in Athabasca; schooling in Manitoba;politics; his activities in French Canadian affairs; propaganda; elections, etc.; covers 1880-1914; copy in Laval University. 675

LAWRENCE, Major Charles (1709-1760). Military journal, April, 1750; military movements in the basin of the Chinecto; and records of the Governor of Nova Scotia.MS, British Museum, Add. 32821, folios 345-350. 676

LAWSON, William (1793-1875, of Brampton, Ont.). The Life of William Lawson (1917). Autobiographical sketch of pioneer who founded Brampton; goes up to his emigration in 1829; a record of boyhood and religious life in Cumberland; Primitive Methodism. Copy in Harvard. 677

LEACOCK, Stephen (1869-1944). The Boy I Left Behind Me (New York, 1946). Early childhood in England, boyhood on a farm near Lake Simcoe; his schooling, study at Upper Canada College, and ten years of teaching at Strathroy Collegiate Institute and in high school. 678

LEAF, Walter (1852-1927).Some Chapters of Autobiography (London, 1932).A scholar's autobiography; it includes a section on travels in Canada. 679

LE BEAU, Claude. Aventures (Amsterdam, 1738) two vols. Charmingly written account of trip to America in 1729;the Huron, Iroquois, and Algonquin Indians of Canada. 680

LE CARON, Major Henri (b. 1841). Twenty five Years in the Secret Service (London, 1892).Soldiering and espionage, especially among Irish nationalists in Canada and U.S.A. 681

LECKY, Peter (pseud.). Peter Lecky, by himself (London 1915). Adventures of a rolling stone; including ranching and mule skinning in Canada before World War I; and his experiences with Indians. 682

LEE, Herbert Patrick. Policing the Top of the World (London, 1928). Service with the North-West Mounted Police at Craig Harbour in the 1920's: crimes, travels, adventures. 683

LEES, John, of Quebec. Travel diary, April-October, 1768; a merchant's trip to New England, New York. and return; descriptions of business conditions, etc. Soc. Colonial Wars Michigan Proc. (Detroit, 1911) 55 pp. 684

LE FROY, Sir John Henry (1817-1890). Diary of a Magnetic Survey (London, 1883). Mostly impersonal record of scientific observations in northwestern Canada, 1842-1844. 685

LEIGHTON, Caroline C. Life at Puget Sound (Boston, 1884). Her travels in the Pacific Northwest, 1865-1868; including British Columbia. 686

LE LOUTRE, Abbé Jean Louis (1709-1772). The Career of the Abbé Le Loutre, by John C. Webster (Shediac, N.B., 1933). Included is a translation of his autobiography of missionary work among the Micmacs of Nova Scotia while he was Vicar-General of Acadia. The work was originally published in Nova Francia VI (1931) 1-34. 687

LENORMAND, Michelle, of Montreal. Autour de la Maison (Montreal, 1918). Sketches of her childhood, family life, games, in Montreal; arranged by seasons. 688

LEONARD, Hon. Elijah (b. 1814). A Memoir (London, Ont. 1894). Life at Long Point in Norfolk County; experiences in rebellion of 1836-1837; removal to London; political commentary; Reform Party; slave rescue. 689

LESLIE, Col. Stephen. Military Journal (Aberdeen, 1887). Account of his military career, 1807-1832; from 1816 in Canada; social life and observations in Halifax and Montreal. 690

ANON. Letters from Muskoka. By an Immigrant Lady (London, 1878). An autobiography, in letter form, of her first years of pioneering life in the Muskoka district, Ontario, in the seventies. 691

LEVINGE, Sir Richard George Augustus (1811-1884). Echoes from the Backwoods (London, 1845). A British soldier's experiences in New Brunswick and Nova Scotia in 1835; and in Upper and Lower Canada during the 1837 rebellion; Indians. 692

LEWIS, Thaddeus (b. 1793). Autobiography (Picton, 1865). War of 1812; life, travels, and work of a Methodist minister in Upper Canada; a vivid record. 693

LIGHT, Colonel A. W. Journal and letters, 1833-1838; farming and settler's life near North Oxford, U. C.; claims of settlers; politics of England and Canada; troubles with Americans; farming details. MS, Ottawa Archives. 694

LIGHTON, William B. (b. 1805). Narrative of the Life of William B. Lighton (Troy, 1846). Childhood in England; military service in Canada; period in military prison in Quebec; escape and flight to U.S.A. A copy in Bibliothèque St. Sulpice. 695

LINDSAY, David Moore. Camp Fire Reminiscences (Boston, 1912). Memories of hunting and fishing, mostly in Quebec province; moose and caribou. 696

LINDSAY, Lieut. William. Military journal, September-December 1775; military details of the siege and blockade of Quebec, by a militiaman. Canadian Rev. II and III (1826). 697

LITTLE, R.H. Reminiscences of My Pioneering Experiences (Treherne, Man., 1931). Experiences of a winter, 1879-1880, in Township 7, Range 12, Cypress River, Manitoba. 698

LITTLEHALES, Major Edward Baker (died 1825). Travel journal, February-March, 1793; journeys with Governor Simcoe through southern Ontario; Indians, Moravians, settlers. London and Middlesex Hist. Soc. Trans. VIII (1917) 6-14 (from Canadian Literary Messenger, 1833). Journal Written by Edward Baker Little (Toronto, 1889). 699

LIVESAY, J. F. B. (d. 1944). The Making of a Canadian (Toronto, 1947). His boyhood in Ireland and England; journalism with the Canadian Press, Toronto; writing for children; in form of essayettes. 700

LIVINGSTONE, F. J. My Escape from the Boers (Toronto, 1900). Adventures of a Canadian medical missionary in South Africa during the Boer War. 701

LLOYD-JONES, Gertrude. "On A Canadian Farm," National Review, June 1910. Reminiscences of twelve years of farming; notes on general social conditions. 702

LOFTHOUSE, Right Rev. Joseph, Bishop of Keewatin. A Thousand Miles from a Post Office (Toronto, 1922). A record of religious work and travel during twenty years in the Hudson Bay Company region. 703

LOFTY (pseud.). Adventures and Misadventures (London, 1922).
An English undergraduate's humourous account of his experiences in Canada, trying to make a living, just before World War I. 704

LOGAN, Sir William Edmond (1798-1875). Scientific journals, 1829-1846; travels in Europe and North America; geological survey of Lake Superior district; geology, copper, and coal mining. MS, Toronto Public Libraries, 4 vols. Excerpts in B. J. Harrington's Life of Sir William E. Logan (Montreal, 1883). 705

[LONDON, M. C. S.]. Travel journal, July 1851-February 1852; an Englishman's journey to New Brunswick; and his experiences alone on the Tobique River. Adventures in Canada (London, 186-?). 706

LONG, John. Voyages and Travels of an Indian Interpreter and Trader (London, 1791; Cleveland, 1904; Chicago, 1922). His life in Canada, 1768-1788; travel and fur-trading in the Nipigon country and northern Quebec; Indian customs and languages; valuable. 707

LONGLEY, James Wilberforce (1849-1922). "Reminiscences," Canadian Mag. LV, LVI, LVII (October 1920-February 1921). His memories of the political and legal affairs in the Maritime provinces from 1871; his work as judge of the Supreme Court of Nova Scotia. 708

LORD, William R. Reminiscences of a Sailor (Glasgow, 1894). A sea-captain's life; includes visits to Quebec. 709

LUARD, Capt. Thomas W. Military diary, 1836-1838; his militia service in the Upper Canada rebellion; the Navy Island campaign. R. and K. M. Lizar, In the Days of the Canada Company (Toronto, 1936). 710

LUMSDEN, James (b. 1854). The Skipper Parson (Toronto, 1906). Experiences of a Methodist minister; among the Newfoundland fishermen; his circuit travels and conversions; lives of the fishermen. 711

LUNDY, Benjamin (1789-1839). Travel journal, 1832; through the western parts of Upper Canada; with the purpose of showing negroes the conditions of life in Canada and the possibilities of emigration. Ontario Hist. Society Papers and Records XIX (1922) 110-133. 712

LYELL, Sir Charles (1797-1875). Travel diary, July 1841-August 1842; thro' New England, Nova Scotia, and Upper Canada; geology, topography, society, celebrities. Travels in North America (London, 1845) 2 vols. 713

LYNCH, Jeremiah. Three Years in the Klondyke (London, 1904). Personal experiences of frontier life and mining during the gold-rush, 1898-1901; violences at Dawson. 714

[LYON, Laurance (1875-1932), author]. By the Waters of Babylon (London, 193-?). Autobiography of a Canadian who lived after 1905 in France and in England and was a member of the British House of Commons;his childhood and his law practice in Canada; World War I; authorship. 715

LYSONS, Sir Daniel (1816-1898). Early Reminiscences (London, 1896). His experience in Canada during the rebellion, 1836-1838; and in Nova Scotia in 1847; general conditions, military life and activities; the backwoods; lively. 716

McALEER, G. Reminiscent and Otherwise (Worcester, Mass.1901). Brief memories of life in eastern Quebec in the 50's. 717

McALPINE, Donald (b.1849). Autobiography, written about 1927. Life of a school teacher, inspector, real estate and loan-company worker. MS, Toronto Public Libraries, 22 pp. (typewritten copy). 718

McALPINE, John. Genuine Narratives and Concise Memoirs (London, 1788). Adventures of a Highlander in North America and Canada; with British armies in Canada and life in Nova Scotia, 1773-1779; losses in the cause. 719

MACAULAY, R. H. H. Trading into Hudson's Bay (Winnipeg,1934). Journal written during a trip to Hudson's Bay in 1934, with Patrick Ashley Cooper, governor of the company. 720

MACAULAY, Robert. Travel journal, August-October, 1815; from Kingston to Montreal, Boston, and New York; a lively narrative and description. MS, Queen's University. 721

McBETH, Roderick George (1858-1934). Making of the Canadian West (Toronto, 1898). Reminiscences of an eye-witness and participant in expansion and development of western Canada and Manitoba. 722

McBRIDE, Captain Herbert Wes. A Rifleman Went to War (Onslow County, N.C., 1935). Personal experiences of an American in the Canadian Army in France, World War I, 1915-1916; on the Somme. The Emma Gees (Indianapolis, 1918). His later experiences as a machine-gunner in France. 723

McCALLUM, Fred H. (1850?-1923). "Experiences of a Queen's Own Rifleman at Ridgeway," Waterloo Hist. Soc., 3rd Annual Report (1915) 24-30. Details of the 1866 Fenian revolt in Canada. 724

McCHARLES, Aeneas (born 1844). Bemocked of Destiny (Toronto, 1908). The struggle and misadventures of a Canadian pioneer from boyhood; teaching, business, farming, in Winnipeg and Ontario; simple, detailed, and interesting. 725

McCLINTOCK, Sergeant Alexander. Best o'Luck (New York, 1917). A Kentucky man's services with the Canadian army during 1st World War: Western Front; the Somme. 726

McCLUNG, Mrs. Nellie Letitia (Mooney) (b. 1873). Clearing in the West (Toronto, 1935). The popular autobiography of her life on the Canadian prairies, until the time of her marriage. The Stream Runs Fast (Toronto, 1945). A continuation; life in Manitoba, and Alberta, 1896-1938; farm life, novel-writing, politics, work for women's rights. 727

McCLURE, Rev. William (1778-1871, of Toronto). Life and Labours, ed. David Savage (Toronto, 1872). Forty years of work of an Ulster Methodist, mostly in Ontario, and his journeys to Australia and British Isles; temperance work; Y.M.C.A.; Irish politics; Daniel O'Connell. 728

McCORMICK, J. Hanna. Lloydminster (London, 1920?). Colonizing in a new settlement in Saskatchewan, 1902-1905; conditions and results. The journal on which this book is based in part (April-May, 1903; on trail with the Barr colonists from Saskatoon to Lloydminster) is owned by the University of Saskatchewan. 729

McCORMICK, William (1784-1840). William McCormick's Trip to Ireland in 1823-1825 (Detroit, 1947, mimeographed). Journal of travels kept by a prominent man from Essex County, Upper Canada, during a trip to Ireland. 730

McCREA, Lieut. Col. R. B. Lost Amid the Fogs (London, 1869). Partly his personal sketches of life in Newfoundland, 1861; conditions of settlers. 731

McDIARMID, Mrs. Margaret A. (Galloway). I Lived in Paradise

(Winnipeg, 1943). The reminiscences of her life in an early Manitoba settlement. 732

McDONALD, Alexander (1762-1842). Private journal, 1799; kept while he was sheriff of Upper Canada; personal affairs; the public celebrations of Nelson's victories. MS, Public Archives, Toronto, 11 pp. 733

McDONALD, Alexander. In Search of El Dorado (London, 1905). His experiences travelling and prospecting in the Klondyke. See also his "Pioneering in the Klondike," Blackwood's Mag., May-July, 1899. 734

McDONALD, Archibald (1790-1853). Travel journal, July-October 1828; a canoe voyage with Sir George Simpson, from Hudson's Bay to the Pacific. Malcolm McLeod (ed.), Peace River (Ottawa, 1872) 1-39. 735

McDONALD, Edward Mortimer (1865-1940, of Pictou). Recollections (Toronto, 1938). His services in the Nova Scotia parliament, 1897-1904, and the Canadian parliament, 1904-1926; dominion and provincial politics, Federal affairs, legislative work, debates. 736

McDONALD, Frank C. The Kaiser's Guest (London, 1918). Personal experiences of a Canadian private; on the Western Front, during World War I: Ypres, Sanctuary Wood; capture, imprisonment in Germany, and escape. 737

MacDONALD, Rev. J. F. L. Private diary, 1899-1941; his education at Queen's University; twelve years in the ministry of the Presbyterian and United churches; retirement. MS, Public Archives, Toronto, 30 vols. 738

McDONALD, Sergeant James. (born 1821?). Travel diary, August-September, 1862; from Red River settlement to York Factory. MS, Toronto Public Libraries. 739

MacDONALD OF GARTH, John (b. 1774?). Autobiographical notes; came to Canada in 1791; partner in North-West Company; his experience in the Canadian fur trade; hunting and trapping; Indians, fights. MS, McGill University, De Lery MacDonald Papers, D.25, 226 pages; photostat in University of Toronto Library. 740

MacDONALD, Ranald (1824-1894). Narrative of His Early Life, ed. W. S. Lewis and N. Murakami (Spokane, 1923). Early life on the Columbia, under the Hudson's Bay Company regime; the whale fisheries of the Pacific; travel to Japan;life on the western frontier, 1824-1894. 741

MacDONALD,William John (1832-1916).A Pioneer (Victoria 1915). Sixty years in British Columbia; Victoria in earlier days; prominent personalities, family affairs, travels, politics; his work as a senator. 742

MacDONNELL, Hon. Alexander (1762-1842, of Toronto).Travel diary, September-October, 1793; accompanying Simcoe from Humber Bay to Matchetache Bay. MS, Toronto Public Libraries; Trans. Canadian Inst. I (1889-1890) 128-139. Private diary, 1799; domestic and business life in Toronto; politics; police. J. E. Middleton and Fred Landon, The Province of Ontario (Toronto, 1927) II, App. A. 1246-1250. 743

MacDONNELL, John (1768-1850). Fur-trader's journals, May-October, 1793, and October, 1793-June 1795; Trading journeys to Assiniboine River; Grand Portage to Lake of the Woods; life of the voyageurs, and of a clerk of the North-West Company. The first is published in, C. M. Gates, Five Fur-Traders of the Northwest (Minneapolis, 1933), 63-119; the second is in L. R. Masson, Les Bourgeois de la Compagnie du Nord-Ouest (Quebec, 1889) I, 283-295. 744

McDONNELL, Colonel John (1728-1810). "A Narrative of the Early Life of Colonel John McDonnell,"Canadian Magazine, 1825. Early experiences of a Jacobite in Canada. 745

MacDONNELL, J. S. Stopping Places (Pasadena, Calif.,1946). An autobiography of a Canadian; boyhood in Toronto at the end of the nineteenth century; schooling, family life, student at Queen's University,service in World War I; later life in California. Copy in University of Toronto Library. 746

McDOUGALL, George Millward (1821-1876). Missionary journals, June 1851-November 1875; work among Indians in Saskatchewan; travels and adventures; life of Blackfeet, Sioux,Crees; smallpox epidemics. John McDougall, George Millward McDougall (Toronto, 1888). 747

McDOUGALL, John (1842-1917). Forest, Lake and Prairie (Toronto, 1895). His first twenty years, in pioneer settlements in Upper Canada; prairie life, winter travels, Indians, and missions.Later works in the same vein are: Saddle,Sled and Snowshoe (Toronto, 1896); Pathfinding on Plain and Prairie

(Toronto, 1898); In the Days of the Red River Rebellion (Toronto, 1903); On Western Trails (Toronto, 1911). Wanderings and pioneering in Saskatchewan and the Canadian north-west; missionary work among Indians; his work with the Hudson Bay Company; the Riel Rebellion; lives of the trappers, traders, settlers, farmers, Indians; naive but valuable. 748

McFARLANE, John (1779-1839?). Travel journal, May-July, 1821; with his family, from Scotland to Quebec and Montreal; settlement at Lanark. MS, Toronto Public Libraries. 749

MacFARLANE, Roderick Ross. Exploration diary, June-July, 1857; expedition down the Anderson River, Mackenzie River district Canadian Record of Science (January, 1890) 28-53. 750

M'GILLIVRAY, Duncan (died 1808). Fur-trader's journal, July 1794-May 1795; journey to Fort St. George, Sask., and winter there; trade, work, traders; Indians and their relation to traders; a good narrative. The Journal of Duncan M'Gillivray, ed. A. S. Morton (Toronto, 1929); MS, Royal Empire Society, London, 88 pp., and University of Toronto. 751

McGILLIVRAY, Simon. Fur-trader's journal, September 1829-May 1830; contents not reported. MS, Alberta Provincial Library, Edmonton. 752

McGILLIVRAY, William. Travel journal, 1794; notes of exploration in northwest Canada. MS, Provincial Library, Victoria, 64 pp. 753

McGREGOR, James (1759-1830). Memoir, by Revd. George Patterson (Philadelphia, 1859). Life of missionary of general synod of Scotland in Pictou, N.S.; based on and including extracts from his autobiography. 754

McKAY, Joseph William. Fur-trader's journal, April-June 1865; from Kamloops to northern British Columbia; factor for the Hudson's Bay Company. MS, Provincial Library, Victoria, 53 pages. 755

M'KEEVOR, Dr. Thomas, of Dublin. Travel journal, June-August, 1812; with Selkirk's expedition to Hudson's Bay; natural history, Indians, Eskimos, adventures. A Voyage to Hudson's Bay (London, 1819). 756

MacKELLAR, Patrick (1717-1778). Military journal, April-September, 1759; military details of the siege of Quebec, by an engineer. Jour. Corps Royal Engineers (1848); reprinted in A.G. Doughty, The Siege of Quebec (1901) V, 33-58.   757

MACKENZIE. Sir Alexander (1764-1820). Exploration journals, June-September, 1789, and October 1792-August, 1793; journeys on behalf of the North-West Company; from Fort Chippewayan to the Arctic in connection with the Northwest Passage, and to the Pacific; the classic of pioneer exploration in the Canadian northwest. Voyages from Montreal (London, 1801), often reprinted. MS, British Museum, Stowe 793 is the basic diary for the first journey.   758

McKENZIE, Alexander. Travel journal, September 1805 to August 1806; from Athabasca to Fort Chippewayan; Great Bears Lake. MS, Provincial Library, Victoria, 42 pp.   759

MACKENZIE, Sir Alexander Campbell (1847-1935). A Musician's Narrative (London, 1927). Including a section on a musical tour in Canada.   760

MACKENZIE, Kenneth. Been Places and Seen Things (London 1935). includes a section on travel and rough experience in Canada Living Rough (London, 1936). His life in Alaska and Aleutians; deported from U.S.A.   761

McKENZIE, Capt. Thomas (born 1830). My Life as a Soldier (St. John, N. B., 1898). His career in the army from the age of eleven; from 1862 in the border militia, and at a school in Fredericton until 1895. Pamphlet in Ottawa Archives.   762

MacKENZIE, W. "Parliament, Press, and People," Westminster Review XXII (1913). Reminiscences of thirty years in the press gallery of the Canadian Parliament.   763

McKERACHER, Rev. D. W. Religious journal, 1873; the work of a Presbyterian minister at Port Arthur and Fort William, Ont. Thunder Bay Hist. Soc. Report XI (1920), 13-18.   764

MacKINLAY, James. Travel diary, May-August, 1890; with Great Fish River exploration party, northward from Great Slave Lake. MS, McGill University, D. 31, and University of Toronto Library (typewritten copies).   765

MacKINNON, Rev. Clarence D. (1868-1937). Reminiscences (Toronto, 1938). Boyhood and education in Scotland; his parish work in Halifax and Winnipeg; teacher and principal at the Pine Hill Divinity School, Halifax; World War I; contemporary ideas.   766

MacKINNON, H. V. War Sketches (Charlottetown, 1901). Personal narrative of services with Canadian forces in the Boer War, 1899-1900. 767

MACKY, Charles. Through the Long Day (London, 1887) two vols. A journalist's life; includes visits to Canada. 768

McLAGLEN, Victor (born 1886). Express to Hollywood (London, 1934). Travels and miscellaneous jobs; includes prospecting and odd jobs in Canada. 769

McLAURIN, C. C. Sixty Years in the Ministry (Edmonton, 1937). Life and work of a Canadian clergyman. 770

McLEAN, John (1799-1890). Notes of a Twenty-five Years' Service (London, 1849) two vols. A classic of wilderness travel in western Canada, Labrador, etc., 1821-1845; Indians, Eskimos; fur-trading in Hudson's Bay area; attacks on the Hudson's Bay Company. Reprinted, ed. W. S. Wallace (Toronto, 1932). 771

McLEOD, Alexander Roderick. Travel journal, September-December, 1831; Hudson Bay Company's employee; journey from Fort Vancouver; recovery of property of Jedediah Smith after the massacre. The Travels of Jedediah Smith (Santa Ana, Calif., 1934) 112-135. 772

McLEOD, Archibald Norman (1796?-1838?). Fur-trader's journal, November 1800-June 1801; at the Swan River Dept. North-West Company; trading between Lake Winnipeg and Assiniboine River; trade, social life, traders, Indians. C. M. Gates, Five Fur-Traders of the Northwest (Minneapolis, 1933). 773

MacLEOD, Sergeant Donald (born 1688). Memoirs (London, 1791). Adventures of a soldier; it includes service under Wolfe at Quebec. 774

McLEOD, John. Fur-trading journals and correspondence, 1812-1844; travel and work of chief trader with the Hudson's Bay Company, in Oregon Territory, etc. MS, Dominion Government Archives; typed transcript in Provincial Library, Victoria, 198 pp. 775

McMICKING, Thomas. Travel diary, 1862; overland from Queenston, C.W., to British Columbia. MS, Alberta Provincial Library, Edmonton. 776

MacMILLAN, Donald Baxter (born 1874). Four Years in the White North (Boston, 1933). Not seen. 777

MacMILLAN, James. Travel journal, June 1827-July 1830; from Fort Vancouver to Fraser's River; the establishment of Fort Langley. MS, Archives British Columbia; typed copy in Provincial Library, Victoria, 209 pp. 778

McMURRAY, Revd. W. Journal of a Mission to England (Toronto, 1869). A record of a trip in 1864 to raise funds on behalf of Trinity College, Toronto; preaching engagements. 779

McNEILL, William H. (1800-1875). Trading journal, 1851; on board the Hudson's Bay Company's brigantine "Una," at Queen Charlotte Islands; trading for gold at Mitchell's Harbour. MS, Provincial Library, Victoria, 17 pp. 780

MACOUN, John (1831-1920). Autobiography (Ottawa, 1922). Life of a naturalist and an explorer, working for the Geological Survey of Canada. Travel journal, 1872; his journey across the Rocky Mountains, on the Cariboo trail; notes on botany and natural history. Philadelphia Geog. Society Bull. XXVIII (1930), 199-210. 781

McPHAIL, Alexander James (1883-1931). Business diary, January 1920-September 1931; account of his years spent organizing the Canadian Wheat Pool. The Diary of Alexander James McPhail, ed. H. A. Innis (Toronto, 1940). 782

MacPHAIL, Sir Andrew (1864-1938). The Master's Wife (Montreal 1939). Charming reminiscences of his family and of his boyhood in Prince Edward Island, up to 1st World War; Scottish settlers; social life, church, education. 783

MacPHERSON, Madame Daniel. Mes Mémoires (Montreal, 1891). Her reminiscences of life in Quebec from 1835; mostly religious, especially of the Ursulines of Quebec. A translation is in McGill University. It is a sequel to her Reminiscences of Old Quebec. 784

MacPHERSON, Stewart. The Mike and I (London, 1948). Autobiography of a Toronto man; broadcaster with B.B.C. 785

McRAYE, Walter, of Merrickville, Ont. Town Hall Tonight (Toronto, n.d.). Travels and reminiscences of a professional entertainer during thirty years; travels through Canada; recitals, lectures, journalism. 786

McROBIE, William Arme. Fighting the Flames (Montreal, 1881).
Twenty-seven years with the Montreal fire brigade and salvage corps; important fires; adventures and escapes. 787

MacTAGGART, John (1791-1830). Three Years in Canada (London, 1829). Experiences of a Scottish engineer building the Rideau Canal, 1826-1828; description and natural history, customs, economics. 788

MacTAVISH, Newton, Ars Longa (Toronto, 1938). Reminiscences of Canadian Painters and painting, from the eighties; clubs and social life in Toronto. 789

McWILLIAMS, Margaret. Manitoba Milestones (London, 1928). Not seen; since found to be history only. 790

MAILLET, Adrienne. Quelle Vie! (Montreal, 1940). Reminiscences of a French-Canadienne: not seen. 791

MAIR, Charles (1838-1927). Travel diary, February-April 1870; Portage La Prairie to Detroit; also various other journals from 1875 to 1922; notes on the birds and animals of western Canada, etc. MS, Queen's University, Kingston, Ont. 792

MAITLAND, S. C. Private journal, 1846; apparently of Canadian interest; not seen. MS, Ottawa Archives. 793

[MAJOR, Mrs. Henniker]. Canadian Life as I Found It: by Homesteader (London, 1908). Experiences as an emigrant farmer in Saskatchewan, 1904-1907; life of the settlers, politics, general conditions. 794

MALARTIC, Anne Joseph Hippolyte de Maures, comte de (1730-1800). Military Journal, April 1755-November 1760; experiences during the French and Indian wars in Canada, while he was aide to Montcalm. Journal des Campagnes au Canada (Paris, 1890). 795

MALHIOT, François Victor (1776-1840). Fur-trading diary, July 1804-June 1805; Fond du Lac Department, North-West Company; life and work at the post; economics of the fur-trade; translated. Wisconsin Hist. Colls. XIX (1910), 163-215. MS, Alberta Provincial Library, Edmonton. 796

MALLET, Capt. Thierry. Glimpses of the Barren Lands (New York 1930). His experiences inspecting fur-trading posts in the far North; Eskimos. 797

MALONE Colonel Dick. **Missing from the Record** (London, 1947).
His service in World War II as liaison officer with Canadian troops in Italy and as public relations officer with the Canadian army in Normandy; role of the Canadians in the war; account of Montgomery. 798

MANION, Robert James (1881-1943). **A Surgeon in Arms** (New York 1918). His service with the Canadian medical corps in France during World War I; Ypres to Vimy Ridge; work in hospitals at the front and in Paris. **Life is an Adventure** (Toronto, 1936). An autobiography of fifty years; life on the prairies, at universities in Canada and England and as a general practitioner, and as an army surgeon; political and public service in Canada after the war. 799

MANNING, Mrs. Ella Wallace (born 1910). **Igloo for the Night** (Toronto, 1946). Her life with her husband in Baffinland in 1938-1941, exploration for Hudson's Bay Company. 800

MANSBRIDGE, Albert (b. 1876). **The Trodden Road** (London 1940). Including a section on his work, lecturing and education in Canada. 801

MARIE SAINTE-CÉCILE DE ROME, mère: (Marguerite-Marie Dina Bélanger, 1897-1929). **Autobiographie** (Quebec, 1938?). Autobiography and journal of religious meditations, by a nun in the convent of Jésus-Marie, Sillery, Que. 802

MARMETTE, Joseph. **Récits et Souvenirs** (Quebec, 1891). Recollections of his trip, from Quebec to Washington and Florida in 1882, and of his trip to France and England; society and political life. 803

MARSH, Robert. **Seven Years of My Life** (Buffalo, 1847). Personal narrative of his part in Upper Canada rebellion of 1838 political affairs; seven years' transportation in Tasmania; pioneer life in Tasmania. 804

[MARSH, William?]. Religious diary, March 1843-January 1845; life and work of a Baptist in Canada. **MS, McMaster University**, 124 pp. 805

MARSHALL, John G. (b. 1786, of Halifax). **Personal Narratives** (Halifax, N.S., 1866). His religious life and God's providences; work and travels in Canada for the temperance movement; his law practice and career as a judge in Cape Breton etc. 806

MARTIN-HARVEY, Sir John. Autobiography (London, 1934). Career of the famous actor; including sections on theatrical tours in Canada. 807

MASCARENE, Paul. Private journal, 1742-1753;contents unknown. MS, Ottawa Archives, Brown Papers, Vol. I. 808

[MASSON, Charles E.]. Gold Nugget Charlie: by Frances Lloyd-Owen (London, 1939). A personal narrative of a gold-miner; compiled from his notes. 809

MATHESON, Alexander (born 1844). Autobiography; an account of his early life, written in 1872. MS, Toronto Public Libraries, 30 pp. Fur-trader's diaries, 1864-1904; in the service of the Hudson's Bay Company, in Winnipeg, Kenora, Nipigon, and Fort William districts; includes memoranda and reflections. MS, Toronto Public Libraries, 12 vols. 810

[MATHEWS, Major Robert]. Military diary, July 1786-July 1787; a journey from Quebec to Detroit and administrative work at the fort there. MS, Public Archives, Ottawa; copy in Toronto Public Libraries. 811

MATTHEWS, Richard F. (b. 1832). Private diary, January 1863-January 1865, and January 1881-March 1899; private affairs of an Irish settler in London, Ont.; home and church life; work at the post office. MS,Toronto Public Libraries (Typewritten copy), 3 vols. 812

[MAUDE, John]. Travel Journal, June-October, 1800; trip from New York to Niagara, Quebec, and return via Lake Champlain; the narrative of an Englishman resident in America.Visit to the Falls of Niagara (London, 1826). 813

MAULEVRIER, Edouard C. V. Colbert, comte de. Voyage dans l' Interieur des États-Unis et au Canada (Baltimore, 1935).Includes tour in Niagara, Ontario, etc. 814

MAXWELL, Henry. Fur-trading journal, 1853-1855; work and travel of chief factor at Dunvegan post, Hudson's Bay Company. MS, Alberta Provincial Library, Edmonton. 815

MAY, Walter William. Sailor's journal, 1852-1853; aboard the Assistance. MS, Ottawa Archives. 816

MAYERHOFFER, Rev. V. P. (b.1784). Twelve Years a Roman Catholic Priest (Toronto, 1861). An Austrian's autobiography of theological training in Europe and his career as a military chaplain; conversion to Protestantism; career as an Anglican clergyman at Whitby, Ont.; anti-Catholic arguments. 817

MAYNE, Richard Charles (1835-1892). Four Years in British Columbia and Vancouver Island (London, 1862). Experiences of a naval lieutenant on duty in British Columbia and Vancouver Island, 1857-1861; natural history, gold fields, and Indians. 818

MELSHEIMER, Rev. Frederick Valentine (1749-1814). A religious journal, February-August 1776; the voyage of a Hessian army chaplain from Wolfenbüttel to Quebec; description of Quebec and environs. Lit. Hist. Soc. Quebec Trans., No. 20 (1891) 137-178. 819

MENDES, D. H. Military diary, December 1917-December 1918; a private in the Canadian Signal Corps; personal experiences in France during World War I. MS, Public Archives, Toronto, 102 pp. 820

MENZIES, Archibald (1754-1842). A scientific travel journal, April-October, 1792; records of a naturalist and surgeon on Vancouver's voyage off the northwest coast;general and scientific notes. Archives British Columbia Memoir V (Victoria 1923) 171 pp. 821

MERRICK, Elliott. True North (London, 1933). American's work at the Grenfell mission in Labrador; marriage, teaching and odd jobs; life of trapper; interesting. 822

MERRIMAN, T. M Religious diary; no dates given; Baptist work in Canada during 19th Century. MS, McMaster University, 217 pages. 823

MERRITT, Hon. William Hamilton (1793-1862). Private journal, 1813-1852 (extracts); his services in the war of 1812; travels in Canada and England; promotion of the Welland Canal and Canadian railroads; legal work; social and family life. J. P. Merritt, Biography of the Hon. W. H. Merritt (St. Catherines, 1875), 21-398 passim. His journal of his service in the Provincial Light Dragoons,along the Detroit-Niagara border during the war of 1812 is published as: A Journal of Events (Hist. Society Brit. North America, St. Catherines, 1863). Prison journal, July-December, 1814; his captivity in New York State, and news of the war. Select British Documents of the Canadian War of 1812 (Toronto, 1928) III pp. 623-648. 824

MERRITT, Mrs. William Hamilton, of Lincoln, Ont. Private diary, from 1850; social and domestic life, visits, religion. J. P. Merritt, Biography of the Hon. W. H. Merritt (St Catherines, 1875), 369 ff. 825

MESSITER, Charles Alston.Sport and Adventures among the North American Indians (London, 1890).Adventures of an Englishman in western Canada and the United States, in the sixties and seventies. 826

METCALFE, Rt. Hon. Charles Theophilus, Lord (1785-1846). Life and Correspondence: by J. W. Kaye (London, 1854). Contains journals of his service as Governor-General. 827

MICKLE, Charles Julius. Travel journal, March-December 1832; voyage from England to Elora, Upper Canada. MS,Toronto Public Libraries, 10 pp. 828

ANON. Middle-Age (London, 1935). Autobiography of an Englishwoman; includes a stay in Canada. 829

MIDDLETON, Clara and J. E. Green Fields Afar (Toronto, 1947). Clara'a reminiscences of her early days in Alberta,1904 on; personal affairs, social life, and life of settlers in Calgary; recorded by her husband. 830

MIDDLETON, Mrs. Margaret (Agar) (1848-1935). "Antique Ontario," Americana (January, 1940), 7-38.An autobiography and family chronicle; life in Ontario before 1885. 831

MILLER, Émile. Travel journal, May 1903-July 1904; account of his trip around the world with a research party; done when he was twelve years old.Mon Voyage Autour du Monde (Montreal, 1926). 832

MILLER, Linus Wilson (1818?-1880). Notes of an Exile (Fredonia, 1846). Personal narrative of his part in the Canadian rebellion of 1838; his trial and transportation; six years' exile in Tasmania. 833

MILLMAN, Thomas. Private diary, 1872-1875; notes of assistant surgeon on the British North American boundary survey; from Lake of the Woods to the Rocky Mountains; notes on western life; topography. Women's Canadian Hist.Soc. Toronto Trans. No. 26 (1928) 15-56. 834

MILLS, George Hamilton (1827-1901). Memoirs of public events and politics in Hamilton. MS, Hamilton Public Library, 441 pp. (typewritten copy). 835

MITCHEL, John. Travel diary, 1764; survey and field notes at Passamaquoddy, N. B. New Brunswick Historical Soc. Colls. V (1904) 175-188. 836

MITCHELL, Benjamin Wiestling (b.1861). Trail Life in the Canadian Rockies (New York, 1924). His nine summers in British Columbia and Saskatchewan; camping; mountain-climbing. 837

MITCHELL, George M., of Quebec. The Golden Grindstone (London 1935). Travels across the northwest and experiences in the Yukon during the 1898 gold-rush; hunting, trading, prospecting, mining, social life; settlement among Indians. Recorded by Angus Graham. 838

MOBERLY, Henry John (born 1835). When Fur Was King (Toronto, 1929). Career as a factor with the Hudson's Bay Company in the northwest; travels, adventure, trading, Indians. 839

MOBERLY, Walter (1832-1915, of Vancouver). The Rocks and Rivers of British Columbia (London, 1885; Ottawa, 1926). His life as a civil engineer in British Columbia, from the fifties to the seventies; his geology and mining. Blazing the Trail through the Rockies: by Noel Robinson and the Old Man Himself (Vancouver News-Advertiser, 1914). Mostly dictated reminiscences of forest clearing, exploration, adventures, in connection with railway building in British Columbia. A pamphlet in Ottawa Archives. 840

MONCK, Frances Elizabeth Owen (Cole) (d. 1919). Travel diary, May 1864-May 1865; account of her travel in Canada; topography, society, and social life. My Canadian Leaves (London, 1891). 841

MONROE, Lieut. Jack. Mopping Up (New York, 1918). Personal narrative of a Canadian soldier's experiences in France during World War I; Western Front and Ypres. 842

MONTAGUE, Sydney R. North to Adventure (New York, 1939); and I Lived with the Eskimos (London, 1940); Riders in Scarlet (Evanston, Ill., 1941). His experiences in the Royal Canadian Mounted Police, upholding the law with the stiff upper lip; Mackenzie district and Port Burwell, Baffin Land, etc. Criminals, dogs, Indians, Eskimos, and Mounties. 843

MONTCALM DE ST. VERAN, Louis Joseph, marquis de (1712-1759). Military journal, 1756-1759; details of military campaigns and activities in Canada; siege of Quebec. H. R. Gasgrain, Guerre du Canada (Quebec, 1895) Vol. VII 844

MONTGOMERY, Colonel Arthur. Reminiscences of service in Canada with the 1st Battalion, 1862-1870. Rifle Brigade Chron., 1911. 845

MONTPETIT, Edouard, of Montreal. Souvenirs (Montreal, 1944), 2 vols. Reminiscences of politics and war and celebrities in Canada and France; World War I. Copy at Laval. 846

MONTRESOR, Capt. John (1736-1799). Military journals, January 1757-December 1778; an English engineer's journeys and campaigns in Canada; Fort Edward, Louisbourg, Quebec, American revolution. New York Hist. Soc. Colls (1881) 11-520; Maine Hist. Soc. Colls. I (1865), 448-466; Trans. Royal Soc. Canada, 3d Ser. XXII (1928) 10-29. 847

MOODIE, John Wedderburn Dunbar (1797-1869). Scenes and Adventures as a Soldier and Settler (Montreal, 1866). Service in the British Army, from 1814; emigration to Canada and pioneer life, 1832-1863; services in 1837 rebellion; farming in Hastings, Ontario, and work as sheriff. 848

MOODIE, Susanna (Strickland) (1803-1885). Roughing It in the Bush (London, 1852); Life in the Clearings (London, 1853). Upper Canada from 1832; personal, social, settlers and pioneers; clearing land, religion, entertainments, social; and visits to Toronto and Niagara. 849

MOODY, H. "Political Experiences in Nova Scotia, 1867-1869," Dalhousie Review, XIV (1934) 65-76. Reminiscences of secretary to Lieut. Governor Doyle; inside story of repeal legislation in Nova Scotia. 850

MOONEY, Daniel (b. 1860). The Travels and Philosophy and Life and Times (Winnipeg, 1930). Autobiography of an Irish exile; a hodge-podge of autobiography and philosophy; spent some time in an asylum; very disordered. 851

MOORE, George (1800-1876). Travel journal, August-November, 1844; the last three months deal with his tour in Upper and Lower Canada, including Niagara Falls. Journal of a Voyage across the Atlantic (London, 1845). 852

MOORE, J. G. Fifteen Months round about Manitoba (Stratford-upon-Avon, 1983). Not seen: copy in British Museum. 853

MOORE, Phil H. With Gun and Rod in Canada (London, 1922). Hunting and fishing in Canada; his life as a guide and professional hunter in Nova Scotia. 854

MORETON, Rev. Julian. <u>Life and Work In Newfoundland</u> (London, 1863). Thirteen years as a missionary at Greenspond; church work; local life and conditions. 855

MORICE, Rev. Adrien Gabriel (1859-1938). <u>Fifty Years in Western Canada</u> (Toronto, 1930). Reminiscences of a missionary priest in western Canada, 1880-1930. 856

MORPHY, E. M., of Toronto. A series of pamphlets: <u>The School upon the Hill</u> (Toronto, 1890); <u>Sainty Smith</u> (Toronto 1890); <u>A York Pioneer Looks Back</u> (Toronto, 1890) and <u>Life Pictures</u> (Toronto, 1893). Reminiscences of his boyhood in York, by the Toronto Jeweller; schools and schoolmasters; settlers odd characters, societies, the rebellion of 1837; pioneers' life. Copies in University of Toronto Library. 857

MORRIS, Elizabeth Keith. <u>An Englishwoman in the Canadian West</u> (Bristol, 1913). Farming, social life, general conditions in Edmonton and the prairies; hospitals, schools and sport; somewhat impersonal. 858

MORRIS, Maurice O'Connor. Travel journal, May-October, 1863; a tour across the Rocky Mountains; topography, people, adventures. <u>Rambles in the Rocky Mountains</u> (London, 1864). 859

MORRIS, Major Roger. Military diary, 1758; journey from Halifax to Cape Sable to round up Acadians. <u>MS, Ottawa Archives,</u> Chalmers MSS, Nova Scotia, fol. 19. 860

MORRIS, Hon. William (1786-1858). Religious travel journal, 1837-1838; mission to England, to present petition from the Presbyterian clergy of Canada concerning church's finances. Ontario Hist. Soc. Papers XXX (1934) 212-262. Religious diary (no dates given); Queen's University, schools, clergy, Reserve dispute, politics, travels in England. <u>MS, Queen's University</u>, Morris Papers. 861

MORRIS, William John (b. 1832). Travel reminiscences of trip in the 1870's; Ontario to Fort Garry (Winnipeg) on a visit to his brother, the Lieutenant-Governor of Manitoba. <u>MS, Toronto Public Libraries</u>, 20 pp. (typewritten copy). 862

MORRISON, E W. B. <u>With the Guns in South Africa</u> (Hamilton, Ontario, 1901). Personal narrative of his service with the Canadian forces in South Africa during the Boer War. 863

MORSE, William Inglis (born 1874). <u>Autobiographical Records</u> (Boston, 1943). Recollections of his boyhood, family life, and education in Nova Scotia; missionary work there; graduate studies at Harvard; parochial labors in Connecticut; to 1905. 864

MORTON, John (1839-1912). John Morton of Trinidad, ed.Sarah E. Morton (Toronto, 1916). Career and journals of a pioneer Canadian Presbyterian missionary among the East Indians in Trinidad. 865

MOSER, Charles (compiler). Reminiscences of the West Coast of Vancouver Island (Kakawis, B.C., 1926). Career of a pioneer Catholic missionary in the remote parts of Vancouver Island during 1874-1899. 866

MOUNIER, Captain Henri, of Quebec. Sea journal, August 1778-June 1779;a Frenchman's log of a journey from Quebec to the Antilles in the brig Commerce. MS, McGill University, Masson MSS., D.33-34. 867

MOUNTAIN, Armine Simcoe Henry (b. 1797). Memoirs and Letters (London, 1857). It includes extracts from his journal; life in Canada and service in British army. 868

MOUNTAIN, Right Rev. George Jehoshaphat (1789-1863, Bishop of Montreal). Religious diaries, September 1824 and September 1826; two journeys to the Gaspé coast, by the archdeacon of lower Canada; intimate details of travels, social life, natural history, Micmac Indians, etc. Rapport de l'Archiviste de..Québec pour 1941-1942 (Quebec, 1942) 301-344. Religious diary, May-August, 1844; the bishop's visitations of North-West American missions; wilderness life, Indians, religion, morals, at Red River. The Journal of the Bishop of Montreal (London, 1845). 869

MUIRHEAD, James Thorburn. Strange to Relate (London, 1937). Adventurous career; including section on his travels on the Canadian prairies. 870

MUNDAY, Mrs. Luta. A Mounty's Wife (London,1930). Autobiography of twenty years in Regina, Winnipeg, and the far north; detachment life with her husband; Indians; woman's view of social and domestic life. 871

MUNN, Captain Henry Toke. Prairie Trails and Arctic By-Ways (London, 1932). The lively narrative of travels and adventures of an Englishman in western Canada from the 1880's to 1920's; a footloose Johannes Factotum; surveying, trading, prospecting, hunting; Klondyke and Arctic. 872

MURPHY, Charles. "Half a Century of Parliament," Canadian Bar Review, VI (1928) 487-496. Reminiscences of Canadian parliament and politics by a member of the Senate. 873

MURPHY, Emily Gowan (Ferguson) (1868-1933). Janey Canuck in the West (London, 1910). Sketches of farming life, domestic work, country life, travels, religion, people, in Saskatchewan and Alberta; is pleasant but rather impersonal. Seeds of Pine: by Janey Canuck (Toronto, 1922). Reminiscences of life in the Canadian west, by a juvenile court judge. 874

MURPHY, George B. (b. 1857). Military diary, March-July 1885; a transport officer's account of a march from Swift Current to Battleford during the Northwest Rebellion. MS, Toronto Public Libraries, 11 pp. (typewritten copy). 875

MURRAY, Alexander Hunter (1818-1874). A fur trader's journal, 1847-1848; descent of the Porcupine River; erection of Fort Yukon; observations on country and inhabitants; a plain account of the fur-trade. Journal of the Yukon, ed. L.J. Burpee (Pubs. Canadian Archives, 1910). 876

MURRAY, General James (1719-1794). Military journal, September 1759-May 1760; an account of military and political affairs after the surrender of Quebec. Lit. Hist. Soc. Quebec Hist. Docs., 3d Ser. No. 4 (1871) 45 pp. Military journal, May-September, 1760; military and naval affairs about Quebec and Montreal. An Historical Journal: by Captain John Knox (Toronto, 1916) III, 306-334; see also, Governor Murray's Journal (Toronto, 1939). 877

MURRAY, John Wilson. Memoirs of a Great Detective (London, 1904). His varied experiences of crime and criminals during thirty years as a detective and inspector of the C.I.D., at Toronto. 878

MYER, Newton A. (b. 1863). Recollections of his life until he was twenty-seven; experiences in London, Ontario, Illinois, Wisconsin, in the Riel Rebellion, Pacific coast and Alaska. MS, Toronto Public Libraries, 21 pp. (typed copy). 879

NASMITH, Colonel George Gallie (born 1877). On the Fringe of the Great Fight (Toronto, 1917). Experiences of senior sanitary officer with Canadian soldiers in France during World War I; training in England; Ypres; gas attacks; some interesting details of sanitary field-and-laboratory work. 880

[NEED, Thomas (b. 1808?)]. Settler's diary, May 1832-September, 1837; notes of an English farmer in Upper Canada, particularly in Peterborough district. Six Years in the Bush (London, 1838). 881

NEILSON, Colonel J. L. H. War journal, 1812-1814; experiences of an officer in the war of 1812; along the border. Queen's Quarterly, II (1894), III (1895). 882

NELSON, George (born 1786). Fur-trader's journals, 1802-1839; a clerk with companies on St. Croix River, Lower Red River, Lake Winnipeg, Moose Lake, Fort William, and English River districts. MS, Toronto Public Libraries, 6 vols. 883

NETTLETON, John. "Reminiscences, 1857-1870," Papers and Records of Huron Inst., II (1914) 13-19. Reminiscences of the settlement of Collingwood, Ont. 884

NEVINS, John Birkbeck (1818-1903). A Narrative of Two Voyages to Hudson's Bay (London, 1847). Voyage in 1842 to York Factory, Hudson's Bay, and in 1843 to Moose Factory, James Bay; notes on Indians and Eskimos. 885

NEWTON, Rev. William (d.1910). Twenty Years on the Saskatchewan (London, 1897). Missionary work in Alberta from 1875; frontier life, emigration, prairies, Indians, Riel's rebellion. 886

NICHOLSON, General Sir Francis (1660-1728). Military journal, July-October, 1710; expedition to and siege of Port Royal; military details. Journal of an Expedition (London, 1711); Nova Scotia Hist. Soc. Colls. I (1879) 59-104. 887

NICHOLSON, J. D. (b. 1863). On the Side of the Law (Edmonton 1944). An autobiography dictated to J.W. Horan; his life in the northwest; service with the Mounted Police. 888

NIVEN, Frederick John (b. 1878). Coloured Spectacles (London, 1938). Apparently of Canadian interest; not seen. 889

NOBBS, Captain Gilbert. Englishman, Kamerad! (London, 1920?). Personal narrative of a Canadian in France during World War I, 1914-1918; the Somme; capture; his experiences in German hospitals and prison camp. 890

NOBLE, Rev. Louis L. After Icebergs with a Painter (New York, 1861). Diary of a summer trip to Newfoundland and Labrador; towns, churches, topography, scenery. 891

NOBLE, Margery Durham, Lady (b. 1828). A Long Life (Newcastle-upon-Tyne, 1925). The earlier part deals with her childhood in Quebec, where her parents owned the Seigneurie of Sainte Cécile de Bec; social life and old scenes in Quebec; later years deal with her life in England. Copy in McGill University Library. 892

NOEL, Norman. Blanket-Stiff (London, 1912). Travels in northern British Columbia; scenery, climate; fruit-farming, logging, ranching, odd jobs; politics. 893

NORDEGG, Martin. "Pioneering in Canada, 1906-1924." Experiences with a pioneer company in virgin land in northern Ontario; Nipissing district; farming and mining. MS, University of Toronto Library, 274 pp. (carbon copy). 894

NORMANDIN, Joseph Laurent. Military journal, 1732; survey of the Quebec area; defensive aspects of topography. MS, photostat, Ottawa Archives. 895

ANON. Notes on the Road: by a Canadian "Guerilla" (Toronto, 1868). Career of a travelling salesman in western Ontario; notes on business, industries, plants, etc.; vigorous comments on travel conditions, hotels, roads, etc. 896

NYE, Thomas (1801-1877, of Montreal). Travel diary, October-December 1837; from Montreal to Chicago, Detroit, Cleveland and back; a lawyer's honeymoon trip; good observations on travel conditions and things and places he saw. Journal of Thomas Nye (Champlain, N.Y., 1932). 897

O'BRIEN, Jack. Into the Jaws of Death (New York 1919). Personal narrative of a Canadian's experience in France during World War I: Somme, Vimy Ridge; capture and escape. 898

O'CALLAGHAN, Sir Desmond. Guns, Gunners, and Others (London, 1925). Autobiography of a military career; includes section on his services in Canada. 899

O'CONNOR, Daniel (1796-1858). Diary and Other Memoirs (Ottawa, 1901). Autobiography of life in Ireland, emigration to America, settlement at By-Town (Ottawa) in 1827. 900

O'DONNELL, John Harrison (b. 1844). Manitoba as I Saw It (Toronto, 1909). Reminiscences of public life and politics in Winnipeg, 1869-1908; Riel's rebellion. 901

OGDEN, Peter Skene (1794-1854). Fur-trader's journals, November 1825-July 1829; Snake River expeditions for the Hudson's Bay Company; fur-trapping, trading, Indian affairs, statistics, geography. Oregon Hist. Society Quar. X (1909) and XI (1910). 902

OGILVIE, William (1846-1912). Exploration journal, September 1895-January 1897; exploration in the Yukon Territory. "Extracts from the Report of an Exploration made in 1896-1897" in The Yukon Territory, ed. F.M. Trimmer (London, 1898) pp. 383-423.   903

O'LEARY, Peter, of London. Travels and Experiences in Canada (London, 1877). A workingman's reminiscences of travel from Montreal to Winnipeg and Chicago and back to Quebec; advice to Irish emigrants.   904

OLIVER, Andrew. A View of Lower Canada (Edinburgh, 1821). Experiences of a man who went to live in Quebec in 1804. The same material, with changed dates, was also published under the title, Travels through Lower Canada: by Thomas Johnston (Edinburgh, 1827).   905

O'MALLEY, James. The Life of James O'Malley (Montreal, 1893). Autobiography of an Irishman in the British army; including his service in Canada, at Montreal and Quebec, where he remained after his discharge. Copy, Ottawa Archives.   906

O'MEARA, Rev. Frederick A.(1814-1888). Religious diary, June-September 1838; his work as a missionary among Indians near Sault Ste. Marie. MS, Public Archives, Toronto, 21 pp.   907

OSGOOD, Thaddeus. A Brief Extract from the Journal (Montreal, 1835). Diary of a Canadian preacher in England, 1829-1835, raising funds for the work of Bible societies among the Indians and destitute settlers of Canada.   908

OSLER, Rev.Featherstone Lake (1805-1895).Records of the Lives of Ellen Free Pickton and Featherstone Lake Osler (Oxford, 1915). Contains autobiography and journals of his education and theological training; ordination and missionary travels and labours in Canada, and social life, to 1839. Religious diaries, April 1839-January 1840; details of visits to Anglican churches in Tecumseth and Gwillimbury. MS, Public archives, Toronto.   909

OSLER, William Henry (b. 1845). Private diary, May 1862-October, 1866; life on a farm at Thornhill, Upper Canada. MS,Toronto Public Libraries, 84 pp.   910

OUTRAM, Sir James (1864-1925). In the Heart of the Canadian Rockies (New York,1906; London, 1933). Canadian clergyman's exploration and climbing; largely impersonal.   911

OWEN, Captain William (1738?-1778).Travel diaries, July 1766-
May 1770 and April-June 1771; a journey along the coasts of
Nova Scotia and Maine;early history of and events in Campo-
bello; an interesting record with substantial entries. New
York Public Library Bulletin,XXXV (1931) passim; New Bruns-
wick Hist. Soc. Colls. I (1894) and II (1899). 912

OXENDEN, Rt. Rev. Ashton (1808-1892, Bishop of Montreal). The
History of My Life (London, 1891).Autobiography of his life
in the ministry; accounts of his parishes and diocese; his
work as Bishop of Montreal from 1869. My First Year in Canada (London, 1871). Experiences in Montreal and Ottawa during the year 1869-1870; religious work, travel, social life
and society. 913

PALLISER, Capt. John (1807-1887). Exploration journals, 1857-
1860; between Saskatchewan River and United States frontier
and the Pacific. Exploration - British North America (London, 1863). 914

PALMER, Rev. Arthur. Diary-report, 1841; notes on conditions
of country and settlers in the south-west part of Upper Canada. MS, Public Archives, Toronto. 915

PALMER, Howard (1883-1944). Mountaineering and Exploration in
the Selkirks (London, 1914). Narrative of pioneer climbing
in the Canadian Rockies, 1908-1912. 916

PALMIERI,Archambault-Palmieri. Mes Souvenirs de Théatre (Montreal, 1944). Reminiscences of a French-Canadian actor from
end of 19th Century; actors, producers, cinema and radio in
Montreal and Quebec Province; anecdotes. 917

PANET, Jean Claude (1720-1778).War diary, May-September 1759;
a detailed military account of the siege of Quebec. Journal
du Siège de Quebec (Québec, 1866). 918

PAPINEAU, L.J. Amédée. Journal d'un Fils de la Liberté (1850)
Political record of the son of the famous Canadian patriot.
MS, Ottawa Archives. 919

PARADIS, J.G. Feuilles de Journal (Quebec, 1923). Memories of
a young country doctor in Quebec Province, 1885-1886; medical work and crises, religious life; strongly Catholic and
patriotic in the French-Canadian movement. Copy in Collection Gagnon, Montreal Public Library. 920

PARENT, Rev. Amand (b. 1818, of Quebec). The Life of the Rev. Amand Parent (Toronto, 1887). An autobiography of a French-Canadian Methodist up to 1875; evangelism; labors among the Oka Indians; attacks on pagan and Catholic idolatry. 921

PARHAM, H.J. A Nature Lover in British Columbia (London 1939). His life in Canada from 1890; ranching in British Columbia from 1905; work, neighbors, Indians, and family; but mostly his observations of birds and wild-fowl. 922

PARKEN, Anna Moroni. Emigranti (Milan, 1907). An Italian autobiography of four years resident in the Muskoka district of Ontario; emigrant life. 923

PARRISH, Maud. Nine Pounds of Luggage (London, 1940). Autobiography of travel and adventure; includes work in dance halls of Nome and Dawson during the Klondyke goldrush. 924

PARSLOE, Muriel Jardine. A Parson's Daughter (London, 1935). Includes a section on her life in Canada after World War I; horsemanship and work with horses. 925

PATTILLO, T. R. Moose-Hunting, Salmon-Fishing, and Other Sketches of Sport (London, 1902). Personal experiences and reminiscences; hunting in Nova Scotia and Canada. 926

PAULI, Frederick G. Chibogamoo (New York, 1907). Journal of a gold-seeking trip from Quebec to Lake Chibogamoo, 1906; his adventures, travel conditions. 927

PEARCE, Richard. Exploration diary, August-December, 1929; a journey into the western Arctic region, Cambridge Bay district; kept by the editor of the "Northern Miner." Marooned in the Arctic (Toronto, 1931). 928

PEARSE, Benjamin William (1832-1902).His reminiscences of the early settlement of Vancouver Island; a lecture by the surveyor-general and commissioner of Land and Works. MS, Provincial Library, Victoria, 13 pp. 929

PEARSON, William Henry (born 1831). Recollections and Records of Toronto of Old (Toronto, 1914). Notes on places, people, vanished things of the mid-nineteenth century; mostly it is impersonal. 930

PEAT, Harold R. Private Peat (Indianapolis, 1917). A personal narrative of service in World War I: in France with the 1st Canadian Division, 1915-1916. 931

PELL, Captain Joshua. Military Journal,April 1776-1777; military details of his services with the British Army in North America; the siege of Quebec. Pelliana (pr.ptd., 1934) Vol. I, No. 1.   932

PELLETIER, Colonel Oscar C. (born 1862, of Quebec). Mémoires, Souvenirs de Famille, et Récits (Quebec, 1940). His boyhood in Quebec, legal studies, his military life with the artillery; Indian skirmishes; special services as commandant of 7th military district of Montreal. Copy in Bibliothèque St. Sulpice.   933

PEMBERTON, Augustus Frederick. Private journal, January 1856-July 1858; notes of his settlement on Vancouver Island; he landed at Victoria in December 1855. MS,Provincial Library, Victoria, 60 pp. (typewritten copy).   934

PENNEFEATHER, John Pyne (d.1913). Thirteen Years on the Prairies (London, 1892). Experiences of an English settler and farmer in Canada, from Winnipeg to Cold Lake.   935

PENNINGTON, Myles (b. 1814). Railways and Other Ways (Toronto 1894). A personal narrative of early days of railroading in England and Canada; sketches of the railroad men he knew. A copy in Bibliothèque St. Sulpice.   936

PERKINS, Simeon (1735-1812). Religious diary, May 1766-March 1780; important record of Connecticut-born Nova Scotian engaged in trading, fishing, lumbering;politics;American privateers. The Diary of Simeon Perkins, ed. Harold A. Innis (Toronto, 1948).   937

PERRAULT, Joseph-François (1753-1844). Biographie (Quebec, 1834). Autobiography of the proto-notary of Quebec, written when he was eighty; journey to America in 1779; Indian experiences; work as translator, merchant, accountant, and protonotary; a simple record. Copy in Bibliothèque St. Sulpice.   938

PETITOT, Émile Fortune Stanislas Joseph (1838-1917). Autobiographical works, as follows: En Route pour la Mer Glaciale (Paris,1887);Autour du Grand Lac des Esclaves (Paris 1891); Quinze Ans sous le Cercle Polaire Arctique (Paris 1889);Les Grands Esquimaux (Paris 1887); Exploration de la Région du Grand Lac des Ours (Paris 1893). The life, religious work, journeys and adventures of a French missionary and explorer in the Canadian northwest, covering years 1862-1882.   939

PFISTER, Charles.   Journal intimate; promoter of École Polytechnique de Montreal. Rev. Trimestrielle Canadienne, XVIII (1931) 348-377.   940

PHIPS, Sir William (1651-1695). Sea journal, August 1690 November 1691; notes of an expedition against Port Royal; details of military and naval operations. A Journal of the Proceedings in the Late Expedition (Boston, 1690).   941

PICKERING, Joseph. Inquiries of an Emigrant (London, 1832). Travels and farming in Upper Canada, 1824-1830; soil, agriculture, customs, opportunities for emigrants.   942

PICKTHALL, Marjorie Lowry (1883-1922). Private journal, 1897-1900; personal records of a Canadian poet and story-writer. MS, Queen's University, Lorne Pierce Collection.   943

PIERCE, William Henry (b.1856). From Potlatch to Pulpit (Vancouver, 1933). Autobiography of a native missionary to the Indians of the north-west coast of British Columbia; Indian life and customs.   944

PIERS, Sir Charles Pigott (b. 1870). Sport and Life in British Columbia (London, 1923). His twelve years of hunting big game and wild fowl; cruising; life in a mining town.   945

PINK, William. Travel diary, 1766-1770; fur-trading journeys for the Hudson's Bay Company in the Quebec area. MS, photostat, University of Toronto Library; original MS in British Museum.   946

PINKERTON, Kathrene Sutherland (Gedney) (b. 1887). Wilderness Wife (London, 1939). With highbrow pioneers, back to nature in the Canadian north; log cabin life;difficulties and triumphs. Three's a Crew (New York, 1940).   Reminiscences of cruising off coast of British Columbia and Alaska. Two Ends to Our Shoestring (New York, 1941).   947

PLESSIS, Mgr.Joseph Octave (1762-1825, Bishop of Quebec).Religious journal, 1811-1812; two journeys to the gulf of the St. Lawrence and the Gaspé peninsula; religious visitation. "Journal de deux voyages Apostoliques," Fay. Canad., 1865. Religious journals, May-September 1815, May-August, 1816; a record of pastoral visits to Nova Scotia and New Brunswick, and to Upper Canada. Journal des Visites Pastorales de 1815 et 1816 (Quebec, 1903). Religious journal, July 1819 to May 1820; journey to France on church affairs; touristic notes with a religious emphasis. MS, Ottawa Archives (transcript made in 1837).   948

POCOCK, Roger. A Frontiersman (London,1903); Chorus to Adventurers (London, 1931). Autobiography of a johannes-factotum laborer, painter, missionary, cowboy, Mounty, miner, pedlar, fisherman, movie-actor and scout from 1880; service in World War I; mostly in Canada. 949

PODMORE, St. Michael. Rambles and Adventures (London, 1909). Includes a section on his Canadian experiences. 950

POLLARD, William Correll (b. 1878). Pioneering in the Prairie West (London, 1933). Experiences as a farmer and settler in the Parry Sound colonies, near Edmonton, in the early nineties. 951

POLLOK, Allan (1829-1918)."Recollections of Sixty Years Ago," Nova Scotia Hist. Soc. Colls. XIX (1918) 17-30. Reminiscences of a Presbyterian clergyman, who went to Nova Scotia in 1852; churches, well-known people, places. 952

POOLE, Francis. Queen Charlotte Islands (London,1872). Adventures of an Englishman in the islands in 1862-1864; Indians and pioneers. 953

POPE, William (1811-1902). Private diary, March 1834-February 1843; from England to Upper Canada thro' New York; his life in Upper Canada; notes and sketches of natural history. MS, Toronto Public Libraries. 954

POUCHOT, Captain. Military journal, July 1759; a French record of military operations in the siege of Niagara; trans. E. B. O'Callaghan, Docs. Rel. Col. Hist., State New York, X (1858) 977-992. 955

[POUTRÉ, Felix (1817?-1885)], Escaped from the Gallows (Montreal, 1862); Echappé de la Potence (Montreal, 1869; 1884). A vivid account of the experiences of a prisoner in the rebellion of 1837 who won freedom by feigning madness. 956

POWELL, T. P. Travel diary, October-December, 1886; his brief notes of a journey across Canada.From Montreal to San Francisco (Montreal, 1887). 957

POWELL, William Dummer (1755-1834). Autobiography; early part in Boston and England; later part, law practice in Montreal and work as chief justice of Upper Canada. MS, Toronto Public Libraries, 46 pp. 958

PRENTICE, Charles (1774-1820). Travel diary, September-October, 1807; records of a newspaper man, going from Massachusetts to Niagara, Queenston, Upper Canada, and return. MS, Toronto Public Libraries. 959

PRESTON, T. R. Three Years' Residence in Canada (London,1840) 2 vols. His work in the government service in Toronto 1837-1839; descriptions of the chief towns, politics, economics, business, public works, land grants, condition of Indians, settlers, etc.; somewhat impersonal. 960

PRESTON, William Thomas Rochester. My Generation of Politics and Politicians (Toronto, 1927). Reminiscences of Liberal Party in Ontario; public life in Canada and England; chief events and personalities; imperial relations. 961

PRIEUR, François-Xavier (1814-1891). Notes d'un Condamné Politique (Montreal,1884); Notes of a Convict of 1838, trans. George Mackaness (Sydney, 1949). His activities in the rebellion of 1837;trial and transportation; his experience in Tasmania and New South Wales to 1846; odd jobs;life of settlers and convicts; return; an interesting record. 962

PRINDLE Rev. Alexander. Methodist diary, 1832-1843; his ministry in the Ancaster and Hamilton districts, Ontario; sermons, accounts, marriages. MS, Victoria College, Toronto, Archives Dept., Pam. T. 123, Pr. 963

PRITCHARD, J. F. (b.1857). "The Rev. J. F. Pritchard's Recollections of Red River and Prince Albert Days," The Canadian North-West Hist. Soc. Pubs. I, No. 3 (1927) 29-36. His life as a child and young man in the west. 964

PROUDFOOT, Rev. William (1787-1851). Religious journal, June 1832-September 1834; the daily labours and parish life of a Presbyterian minister at London, Ont.; social life, family, personal affairs. London and Middlesex Hist. Soc. Trans. VI (1915), VIII (1917), XI (1922). A religious journal, March 1833-December 1835; his work, visits,travels, general affairs, social life; parochial life and labors among Scotch-Canadians at London. Ontario Hist. Soc. Papers and Records XXVII-XXIX (1931-1933). 965

PROULX DIT CLÉMENT, Jean Baptiste (1846-1904). Religious diary, July-August 1881; in letter form; missionary tour with the Bishop of Ottawa, north of Ottawa River. Au Lac Abbitibi (Montreal, 1885). Religious journal, June-August, 1884;

his first pastoral visit, from Pembroke to Hudson's Bay and return. A la Baie d'Hudson (Montreal, 1886). 966

PROWSE, D. W. "Reminiscences of a Canadian Judge," Canadian Mag., September 1912. His early days and law experiences in Newfoundland. 967

PUGET, Lieut. Peter (1764?-1822). Sea journal, May-June 1792; with Vancouver during the exploration of Puget Sound; topography and natural history. Pacific Northwest Quarterly XXX (1939) 177-217. 968

PUGSLEY, Lieut. William H. Saints, Devils, and Ordinary Seamen (Toronto, 1945). Life on the lower deck in the Canadian Navy; service in World War I and afterwards; in Canadian waters and at Scapa Flow. 969

PUTNAM, John Harold (b. 1866). Fifty Years at School (Toronto 1938). The reminiscences of a teacher in Toronto and Ottawa from 1887; advice on pedagogy. 970

PYKE, Magnus. Go West, Young Men, Go West (Ottawa, 1930). His life in Vancouver as a young man out from England; critical views on the economic potential of Canada. 971

PYNE, Rev. Alexander. Reminiscences of Colonial Life (London, 1875). Missionary labors among Indians in Upper Canada; the life and customs and spiritual desolation of Canada. 972

RADISSON, Pierre Esprit (1620?-1710). Voyages (Boston, 1885). Account of travels and adventures, 1652-1684, west of Great Lakes, to the Mississippi, Hudson's Bay, etc. 973

RAE, Herbert. Maple Leaves in Flanders Fields (Toronto,1918?) Personal narrative of his service as an officer in Canadian forces during World War I; Western Front; St. Julian; lively record with obscured names. 974

RAE, John (1813-1893). Exploration journal, June 1846-September 1847; record of expedition sent out by the Hudson's Bay Company into the Arctic. Narrative of an Expedition to the Shores of the Arctic Sea (London, 1850). 975

RAND, S. T. A Short Account of the Lord's Work among the Micmac Indians (Halifax, 1873). Missionary labors in Nova Scotia. 976

RANDELL, Jack (b. 1879). I'm Alone (Indianapolis, 1930). Dictated autobiography; a boyhood in Newfoundland; adventurous life in Boer War, 1st World War, and at sea; sinking of the "I'm Alone."　977

RANKEN, George (1828-1856). Canada and the Crimea (London, 1862). Reminiscences of military service; including a period in Canada.　978

RANKIN, Charles (1797-1886). Survey diaries, 1832-1837; brief records of five surveys in Upper Canada. MS, Toronto Public Libraries, 5 vols.; Ontario Hist.Society Papers and Records XXVII (1931) 497-510.　979

RAPER, Fred. Klondyke to Kenya (London, 1938). His travels in northwest Canada; Moose Jaw, Klondyke, Yukon.　980

RAWLE, William, of Philadelphia. Travel diary, 1810; an American lawyer's journey thro' Lower Canada;notes on law, lawyers, constitution, etc. Canadian Hist. Rev. IX (1928) 38-45.　981

RAYMOND, Gérard (1912-1932, of Quebec). Religious diary, December 1927-December 1931; a repetition of pious reflections and devotions by a saintly young Catholic. Journal de Gérard Raymond (Quebec, 1937). A copy in Bibliothèque St. Sulpice.　982

REID, William (born 1880). Memories of Pioneer Days at Pilot Mound (Pilot Mound, Man., 1930). Not seen, but since found to be general essays.　983

ANON. Reminiscences of a Stonemason: by Working Man (London 1908). Autobiography of a wandering life: includes section on his experiences as a laborer in Canada.　984

REMITS, Ernest Lorand (born 1901). Jottings from the New and Old Countries (Ottawa, 1935). Reminiscences of a Hungarian-born Canadian; travel around the world; his life in British Columbia.　985

RICCI, Victor H. Ups and Downs in Canada (Amersham, England, 1922). The slight autobiography of an Englishman who spent twenty-two years in Canada; a copy in Toronto Public Libraries.　986

RICHARDSON, Mrs. Evelyn M. (Fox) (born 1902). We Keep a Light (Toronto, 1945). Autobiography of the keeper of the lighthouse at Bon Portage Island, Nova Scotia; work,island life, family and domestic affairs, visitors, adventures.　987

RICHARDSON, George (d. 1912). Religious diary and memorandum book (no dates given); work of a Baptist in Canada. MS, McMaster University, 90 pp. 988

RICHARDSON, Lieut. James. "Reminiscences," Women's Canadian Hist. Soc. Toronto Trans. XV (1916). Notes of a naval officer in the war of 1812; activities in settlements near Lake Ontario. 989

RICHARDSON, James Henry (1823-1910, of Toronto). Reminiscences, 1829-1905; medical work and the medical profession; in Toronto. MS, Toronto Public Libraries, Robertson Collection (typewritten copy). 990

RICHARDSON, Major John (1796-1852). Personal Memoirs (Quebec, 1838); Eight Years in Canada (Montreal, 1847). A Canadian-born soldier; his military service in Spain with General De Lacy Evans; later service and travel in Canada; 1837 Rebellion; travel, hunting, politics, scenery and towns. 991

RICHARDSON, Sir John (1787-1865). Exploration diary, June-September 1848; through Prince Rupert's Land searching for the Franklin discovery ships; Eskimos, natural history, details of an unsuccessful search. Arctic Searching Expedition (London, 1851) 2 vols. 992

RICHARDSON, Lieut. William (1748-1772). Sea journal, 1771; an account of Labrador during his visit there; surveying work. Canadian Hist. Rev. XVI (1935) 54-61. 993

RICKMAN, Thomas M. Travel diary, August-September 1885; journey of an architect from England to Quebec and Ontario, and later in U. S. A. Notes of a Short Visit to Canada and the States (London, 1886). 994

RIDDELL, Walter (1814-1904). Religious journal, April-August, 1833; journey from Scotland to Cobourg, Ontario; Presbyterian church there; later his ministry in Canada, up to 1900. Diary of a Voyage from Scotland (Toronto, 1932). MS, Public Archives, Toronto. 995

RIDOUT, Thomas (1754-1829, of Toronto). Ten Years of Upper Canada, ed. Matilda Edgar (Toronto, 1890). Journal letters covering 1805-1815; the war of 1812; skirmishes on the Ontario border; society and social life in Upper Canada; travel in England. 996

RITCHIE, James Ewing. To Canada with Emigrants (London 1885)

Across Canada with a party of boys intending to be farmers; prairies and the west; opportunities for emigrants. 997

ROBERTS, Lloyd. The Book of Roberts (Toronto, 1923). Reminiscences of trivia; nostalgic recollections of childhood and family life in one of the maritime provinces. 998

ROBERTS, M. On the Old Trail (London, 1927). Reminiscences of British Columbia in the old days, during a journey taken 40 years later. 999

ROBERTSON, William Norrie (b. 1855). Yukon Memories (Toronto, 1930). A miscellany of anecdotes, letters, and diary, mainly about the Yukon in the nineties; life as a sourdough, adventures, mining, sport. 1000

ROBIN, John (b. 1840). Leaves from a Hobo's Diary (Montreal, 1911). The wandering lifetime of a homeless man; mostly on shipboard; in many parts of the world. Copy in Bibliotheque St. Sulpice. 1001

ROBINSON, Edward Colpitts. In an Unknown Land (London, 1909). travel and prospecting for gold; in the interior of Labrador; Indian life and work. 1002

ROBINSON, Admiral H. Naval journal, 1820; kept on H.M.S. "Favourite" on the Newfoundland station. Royal Geog. Soc. Jour. IV (1834) 207-220. 1003

ROBINSON, Henry M. The Great Fur Land (London, 1879). Trading with the Hudson's Bay Company, in western Canada; journeys, Indians, life in the forts. 1004

ROBINSON, Sir John Beverley (1791-1863, of Toronto). Private diary, 1838-1840 and 1855; kept in England; notes on political and legislative matters relating to Canada; a society life with the ruling group in England; Wellington, Russell, Dickens, C. W. Robinson, Life of Sir John Beverley Robinson (Toronto, 1904) 274-389 passim. 1005

ROBINSON, John Beverley (1821-1896, of Toronto). Travel diary May 1851; a Canadian public man's trip to Virginia. MS, Public Archives, Toronto. 1006

ROBINSON, William B. (1797-1873). Public diary, April-September 1850; a journey to Indians at Garden River to treat for lands. MS, Public Archives, Toronto, 32 pp. 1007

ROBSON, Elizabeth. Early Days in Canada (London, 1939). Experiences of a Scottish girl who came to Acton, Ontario, with her family in the early days; reminiscences written for her grandchildren. 1008

ROBSON, Joseph. An Account of Six Years' Residence in Hudson's Bay (London, 1752). Life of a surveyor and building inspector with the Hudson's Bay Company, 1733-1736 and 1744-1747; fur-trade, whaling, seal-trapping. 1009

ROEBUCK, John Arthur (1802-1879). Life and Letters, ed. R. E. Leader (London, 1897). Includes a fragment of autobiography of which part relates to his life in Canada, 1815-1824; on a farm near Toronto; also a diary in England. 1010

ROGERS, Sir John Godfrey (1850-1922). Sport in Vancouver and Newfoundland (London, 1912). Adventures on two holidays in 1908 and 1910; travels, hunting, fishing; partly in journal form. 1011

ROGERS, Colonel Robert D. (1809-1885). Military journal, December 1837-January 1838; the operations and movements of the militia during the rebellion. Canadian Hist.Rev.XIII (1932) 429-430. MS, Public Archives, Toronto. 1012

ROMANET, Louis. Kabluk of the Eskimos: by Lowell J. Thomas (Boston, 1932). Dictated autobiography; his emigration from France to western Canada and to Alaska; his friendship with Eskimos on Koksook River; service in World War I. 1013

ROSE, Hilda. The Stump Farm (Boston, 1928). An excellent record of pioneer farming in Alberta, 1918-1927; her struggles; domestic and family life. 1014

ROSS, Alexander Milton (1832-1897). Recollections and Experiences of an Abolitionist from 1855 to 1865 (Toronto, 1875). Memoirs of a Reformer (Toronto, 1893). The work of a well-known Ontario naturalist in the anti-slavery movement, from 1855-1892; John Brown and the abolitionists; also crusades against liquor and vaccination. 1015

ROSS, Sir George W., of Toronto. Getting into Parliament (Toronto, 1913). Covers 1867-1883; his career as inspector of schools and Minister of Education; parliamentary and political affairs in Canada. 1016

ROSS, Philip Dansken (born 1858). Retrospects of a Newspaper Person (Toronto, 1931). Reminiscences of politics and public life and public men in Canada; work for the Ottawa "Evening Journal." 1017

ROSSEL, Louis-Auguste. Military journal, 1757; military operations in a French campaign to Ile Royale. Rapport de l'Archiviste de...Québec pour 1931-1932, pp. 367-387. 1018

ROULEAU, Charles Edmond (1841-1926). Souvenirs de Voyage d'un Soldat de Pie IX (Quebec, 1881). Journey to Rome, and experiences as a Papal zouave; French-Canadian. 1019

ROURKE, Douglas Musgrave. Private diary, September 1924-January 1927; work as accountant with the Hudson's Bay Company at Fort Chipewayan, Lake Athabasca. Louise Rourke, The Land of the Frozen Tide (London, 1928) 326-352. 1020

ROURKE, Mrs. Louise. The Land of the Frozen Tide (London 1928). Two years at Fort Chipewayan on Lake Athabasca with husband (an accountant working for the Hudson's Bay Company); domestic life; Indians. 1021

ROUSE, John James (b. 1869). Pioneer Work in Canada (Kilmarnock, Scotland, 1935). Autobiography of a Protestant missionary in Ontario and western Canada. A copy in Toronto Public Libraries. 1022

ROWAN, John J. Emigrant and Sportsman in Canada (London, 1876). Reminiscences of a settler; Canadian social life, prairies, farming, sport. 1023

RUNDLE, Sergeant Edwin George (b.1838). A Soldier's Life (Toronto, 1909). His military career; Fenian troubles in Canada, 1866; garrison and barrack life in Halifax and Winnipeg; social life. 1024

RUNDLE, Rev. Robert Terrill. Religious diary, March 1840-September 1848; work of the first Protestant missionary to Alberta. MS, Alberta Provincial Library, Edmonton. 1025

RUSSELL, Benjamin (born 1849). Autobiography (Halifax, 1932). Life and work, judge of the Supreme Court of Nova Scotia and professor of law at Dalhousie University; law and politics; public affairs. See also, "Reminiscences of the Nova Scotia Judiciary," Dalhousie Review V (1926) 499-512. 1026

RUSSELL, George Stanley (b. 1883). The Road behind Me (Toronto, 1936). Autobiography of a United Church minister of Toronto; boyhood in Scotland; work and experiences in England and Canada. 1027

RUSSELL, Peter (1733-1808). Travel diary, 1754-1755; journey to Barbary and later to North America. War journals, July-September 1778 and June 1778-January 1779; relative to the

American Revolution; kept by the Inspector-General of Upper Canada. MS, Public Archives, Toronto. Journal, July 1797-August 1799; land granting in Upper Canada. MS,Toronto Public Libraries, 24 pp. 1028

RUSSELL, Richard (d.1786). Private diary, January-March 1771; personal affairs in Canada; brief notes. MS,Public Archives Toronto. 1029

RYAN, Norman J. Red Ryan's Rhymes and Episodes (1924?). Poems and reminiscences of a Canadian burglar and hold-up man; a sentimental account of boyhood, crimes, and prisons; dictated. 1030

RYERSON, Doctor Adolphus Egerton (1803-1882). The Story of My Life (Toronto, 1883). Sixty years of public service in education; principal of Victoria College, Toronto; sketches of Head, Durham, Metcalfe, etc.; compiled from private records by his executor. 1031

RYERSON, Geoffrey Parker. Memoirs of a Canadian Secretary (Toronto, 1928). A short record of political opinions on English policies, Canadian government, French-Canadians, elections in New Brunswick. Copy in Collection Gagnon, Montreal Public Library. 1032

RYERSON, George Sterling (b. 1855, of Toronto). Looking Backward (Toronto, 1924). Education in Toronto and Europe; experiences as an army doctor in Canada; 1885 rebellion; Boer War; World War I; Red Cross; Canadian politics. 1033

RYERSON, John (1800-1878). Missionary diary, June 1854-February 1855; from Kingston,Ontario,to Red River Settlement and to the Hudson's Bay territory;thence to England by the Hudson's Bay route. Hudson's Bay;or, A Missionary Tour (Toronto, 1855). 1034

SAGARD-THÉODAT, Gabriel (d. 1650). Le Grand Voyage du Pays des Hurons (Paris, 1632), several editions; translated as, The Long Journey to the Country of the Hurons,ed.George M.Wrong (Toronto, 1939). Adventures on a journey, 1623-1624; Indian customs. 1035

SAINT-LUC DE LA CORNE, M. Journal du Voyage (Quebec, 1863). "Shipwreck of L'Auguste" in the St. Lawrence, 1761. 1036

ST. MAUR, Mrs. Algernon (Baroness Seymour). Impressions of a

Tenderfoot.(London, 1890). A hunting trip, 1889; Toronto to Vancouver; social life, economics, lumber camps. 1037

SALLOWS, Rev. Edward (1813-1892). Religious diary, June 1848-June 1849; a Methodist minister's circuit journeys and work in Ontario and Manitoba; Moravians, Indians, pioneering and frontier conditions; lively details. Royal Soc.Canada Proc. 3d Ser., XXV (1931), Sec. 2, 151-163; MS, Victoria College, Toronto, Archives Dept., Pam. T. 123, Sal. 1038

SALUSBURY, John. Private diary, July 1749-March 1753; public affairs in Nova Scotia, where he was a government official; military affairs, Indians, travels, domestic matters, Council, official work and difficulties; kept by a relation of Mrs.H.Thrale and the MS has notes in the writing of Samuel Johnson. MS, John Rylands Library, Manchester, England, 615 (eight small note-books). 1039

SALVERSON, Laura Goodman (born 1890). Confessions of an Immigrant's Daughter (London, 1939). Her girlhood on the Canadian prairie and in Minnesota; servant, clerk, housewife; life among Scandinavian settlers in Saskatchewan; beginnings as a novelist. 1040

SANGUINE, T. M. War diary, 1775; a French eye-witness's notes on the invasion of Canada by the Americans. H. A. Verreau (ed.), Invasion du Canada (Montreal, 1870), 1-156. 1041

SANSOM, Joseph. Travels in Lower Canada (London, 1820). Diary notes on settlers, farming, religion, social life, institutions, etc. 1042

SCADDING, Rev. Henry (1813-1901, of Toronto). Private diary, 1837-1838; the extracts mostly relating to the rebellion in Lower Canada. Women's Canadian Hist. Soc. Toronto Trans.No. 6 (1906). Religious journal, 1883-1889; his work as a tutor and clergyman in Quebec; teaching at Upper Canada College; rector and canon in Toronto. MS, Toronto Public Libraries, 10 vols. 1043

SCHAFFER, Mrs. Mary Townsend (Sharples) (b. 1861). Old Indian Trails (London, 1911). Record of two years of travel, camp, and trail life, in the Canadian Rocky Mountains. 1044

SCHULTE, Paul (born 1896). The Flying Priest over the Arctic (New York, 1940). Four years' work of missionary and priest of the Oblates of Mary Immaculate; introduction of airplane into missionary work in the Arctic. 1045

SCHUSTER, Anselm (1834?-1885). **Life and Labours of Rev. Anselm Schuster**, ed. David Mitchell (Belleville, Ont., 1886). Autobiography and writing of a Belleville missionary, a Jew converted to Christianity. Copy, Toronto Public Library. 1046

SCOTT, Alexander Hugh (b. 1853). **Ten Years in My First Charge** (Toronto, 1891). Autobiography of the Presbyterian minister of Owen Sound, Ontario, stressing spiritual life and ministerial work. Copy in Toronto Public Library. 1047

SCOTT, Canon Frederick George (1861-1944). **The Great War as I Saw It** (Toronto, 1922). A narrative of personal experiences as senior chaplain of the 1st Canadian Division; on Western Front during World War I; heroism of comrades. 1048

SCUDAMORE, Thomas Venables (b. 1889). **Lighter Episodes in the Life of a Prisoner of War** (Aldershot, 1933). Apparently was Canadian prisoner-of-war, World War I; not seen. 1049

SECRETAN, J. H. E. **Out West** (Ottawa, 1910). Reminiscences and sketches of settlers, police, prospectors, Indians, in western Canada. Copy in Queen's University Library. 1050

SELKIRK, Thomas Douglas, 5th Earl of (1771-1820). Private diary, August- November 1803; very full details on settlements and settlers in New York and Massachusetts; notes made preliminary to his own settlement, on farming, economics, law, prices, resources, etc. MS, Ottawa Archives (a transcript); private diaries, November 1803-December 1804; kept in Upper and Lower Canada; brief selections about the foundation of his own settlement. Royal Soc. Canada Proc. and Trans., 3d Ser. VI (1912) Sec. II, 3-9; MS, Public Library, Charlottetown, P.E.I., covers 1803-1804 and relates to settlement in Prince Edward Island. 1051

SELLAR, Gordon (b. 1812?). **Narrative of Gordon Sellar** (Huntingdon, Q., 1915). Autobiography of a Scottish lad who emigrated to Canada in 1825 and settled in Ontario, near Toronto; his work farming; a very good narrative. 1052

SELOUS, Frederick Courteney (1851-1917). **Recent Hunting Trips in British North America** (London, 1907). Experiences hunting in Newfoundland, Yukon, and northern Ontario, from 1900 to 1906. 1053

SELWYN, Alfred Richard Cecil (born 1824). Exploration journal 1870?; report of preliminary explorations and notes on the natural history of British Columbia. Canadian Geolog. Survey Report (1871-1872) 16-72. 1054

SEMMENS, Rev. John. The Field and the Work (Toronto, 1884). Reminiscences; missionary labors in Saskatchewan and Manitoba, from 1874; Methodist preaching and travel; the Red River; traders, Indians, missionaries; sketches. 1055

SERVICE, Robert William (b. 1876). Ploughman of the Moon (New York, 1945); Harper of Heaven (London, 1948). Autobiography of a popular poet; boyhood in England; travels and odd jobs in California, British Columbia, and the Yukon; bank clerk; the spell of the Yukon and his life there, during the gold-rush; travels in America and Europe; his poems and literary success. 1056

SETON, Ernest Thompson (b. 1860). Trail of an Artist Naturalist (New York, 1940). His boyhood in Toronto, and experiences and natural history studies on the prairies; travels to Europe. 1057

SETON-KARR, W. H. Ten Years' Wild Sports in Foreign Lands (London, 1889).Reminiscences of travel and hunting; including section on the Rocky Mountains, hunting big game in the eighties. 1058

SHANNON, S. Leonard. "Twas Fifty Years Ago," Dalhousie Review X (1931). Reminiscences of politics and public affairs by a former parliament clerk;the affairs of the maritime provinces. 1059

SHEEPSHANKS, Rev.John (1834-1912). A Bishop in the Rough (New York,1909). Reminiscences of his early years; parochial and missionary work and travels in western Canada. 1060

SHELDON, Charles (1867-1928). The Wilderness of the Upper Yukon (Toronto, 1911) and The Wilderness of the North Pacific Coast Islands (Toronto, 1912). Some hunting experiences in the Pacific northwest; scientific travels in unknown lands; wapiti, bears, caribou, in British Columbia, Yukon, Alaska, etc. 1061

SHEPHERD, Richard Herne (1842-1895). Account of three months in Newfoundland, 1861, by a British bibliographer; personal affairs, list of poems published in Newfoundland papers.MS, Toronto Public Libraries, 9 pp. 1062

SHERK, Michael Gonder (1862?-1927). "My Recollections of the Fenian Raid," Welland County Hist. Society Papers II (1926) 60-65. His experiences as a child at the time of the Fenian raids. 1063

SHIELDS, John. "Memoirs," Journal of History (Lamonie, Iowa) XII (1919), 448-455. His work and experiences of religious life in the Mormon church in Ontario. 1064

SHORTT, Adam. Private diary, 1779-1810; life and work of farmer, pioneering in Ontario. "Life of a Settler in Western Canada," Bulletin of Dept. Hist., Queen's University, July, 1914; Queen's Quarterly, XXI (July, 1914) 71-88. 1065

SHUTTLEWORTH, T. M. A Tour in Canada and the United States of America (Preston, 1884). Diary of a trip from England,1884; Quebec, Montreal, Niagara, etc.;his views of towns, people, general conditions. Copy at Harvard. 1066

SIBBALD, Mrs. Susan (Mein) (1783-1866). The Memoirs of Susan Sibbald (London,1925). Reminiscences of social and domestic life in Upper Canada, 1856-1866. 1067

SILVY, Father Antoine (1638-1711). Travel journal, July 1684-1685; a Jesuit's journey from Belle Isle to Fort Nelson; in French and English. Documents Relating to the Early History of Hudson Bay, ed.J.B.Tyrrell (Toronto,1931) 35-101. 1068

SIMCOE, Mrs. Elizabeth Posthuma (Gwillim) (1766-1850). Private diary, September 1791-October 1796; kept while her husband was Lieutenant-Governor of Upper Canada; social, domestic, and pioneer life in Canada; an interesting document. The Diary of Mrs. John Graves Simcoe, ed. J. R. Robertson, (Toronto, 1911). 1069

SIMCOE, John Graves (1752-1806). Military diary,October 1777-December 1782; a detailed account of operations and battles with the Queen's Rangers in the American Revolution.Simcoe's Military Journal (New York, 1849). 1070

SIME, Jessie Georgina (b. 1880, of Midlothian). In a Canadian Shack (London, 1937). Reminiscences of impoverished country life among French-Canadians in Quebec; domestic, social,and religious. 1071

SIMMONDS, James (1847-1915). Private journal, November 1852-June 1909;his family and private affairs in Dartmouth, Nova Scotia. Frank W. Simmonds, John and Susan Simmonds (Rutland Vermont, 1940) 100-104. 1072

SIMMONS, Mervin C. Three Times and Out: by Nellie L. McClung (Boston, 1918). Dictated reminiscences of a Canadian volunteer in France during World War I; captured; experiences in various German prison camps, escape. 1073

SIMPSON, Sir George (1792-1860). Fur-trader's journal, July 1820-June 1821; his work and travels during his early service with the Hudson's Bay Company, chiefly in the Athabasca department; a personal and revealing record. Journal of Occurrences in the Athabasca Department, ed. E. E. Rich (Toronto, 1938). Fur-trading journal, August 1824-June 1825; a voyage from York Factory to Fort George and return. Frederick Merk, Fur Trade and Empire (Boston, 1931) 3-174. Travel journal, 1841-1842; a tour of inspection of the properties of the Hudson's Bay Company while he was governor; notes of a world tour. Narrative of a Journey round the World (London, 1847) 2 vols. 1074

SIMPSON, Thomas (1808-1840). Travel journal, December 1836-February 1839; the survey of the northern shores of America for the Hudson's Bay Company; geography, topography, natural history, Indians, Eskimos, adventures; lively. Narrative of Discoveries, ed. A. Simpson (London, 1843). 1075

SINCLAIR, Mr. Travel journal, October 1816-August 1817; notes of a passage up Hays River. MS, Alberta Provincial Library, Edmonton. 1076

SINCLAIR, Alexander (1828-1897). Pioneer Reminiscences (Toronto, 1898). His reminiscences of pioneer farming in Ontario from the thirties; historical reminiscences of government. Pamphlet in University of Toronto Library. 1077

SINCLAIR, Gordon. Footloose in India (London, 1933); Signposts to Adventure (Toronto, 1947). A Toronto journalist's adventures and travel in India and many other parts of the world seeking violence, horror, and romance. 1078

SING, Josiah Gershom (1857-1921). Private diary, January 1887-September 1889; a surveyor's notes on everyday happenings, weather, in the Meaford district, Ontario. MS, Toronto Public Libraries, 39 pp. 1079

SINGER, F. B. Souvenirs d'un Exilé Canadien (Montreal, 1871). Not seen: copy in Bibliothèque St. Sulpice. Fiction? 1080

SINTON, Robert (b. 1854). Looking Backward from the Eightieth Milestone (Regina, 1935; mimeographed). Farming at Regina from 1878; pioneer life; agriculture; leadership in agricultural societies. Copy at University of Saskatchewan. 1081

SIPPI, Charles Augustus (born 1844). Private journal, January 1893-December 1897; family and church affairs; work as doctor at the London Insane Asylum, London, Ont. MS, Toronto Public Libraries, 193 pp. (typewritten copy). 1082

ANON. Six Years in the Bush (London, 1838). Experiences of an English settler and farmer in the Toronto region during the thirties. 1083

SKEAD, Captain Francis. Private diary, 1850-1851; kept during the expedition in search for Franklin's Polar expedition. MS, owned by C. H. Skead, Esq., Highlands, Post Bag, Grahamstown, South Africa. 1084

SLANEY, Robert Aglionby (1792-1862). Travel journal, August-October, 1860; his journey through Upper and Lower Canada, and then into the U.S.A.; social conditions, topography, and customs. Short Journal of a Visit to Canada and the States of America (London, 1861). 1085

SLATER, James. Three Years under the Canadian Flag as a Cavalry Officer (London, 1893). Political scandals in Toronto; a record of political maneuvers and tampering with documents; Slater held in prison. 1086

SLEIGH, Burrows Willcocks Arthur (1821-1869). Pine Forests and Hacmatack Clearings (London, 1853). Experiences of a military officer in Nova Scotia, New Brunswick, Prince Edward Island, and Lower Canada; social and political conditions; only part personal. 1087

SMADES, Elijah. Private diary, April 1840-March 1841; business, weather, local events at Ogdensburg, N.Y.; kept by a descendant of Justus Sherwood. MS, Public Archives, Toronto. 1088

SMALL, Rev. T. J. Methodist diary, February 1912-April 1915; his work at West Hall, Manitoba; his reading and his reflections on Darwinism and a variety of social and philosophical matters. MS, Victoria College, Toronto, Archives Dept., Pam. T. 123, Sm., 2 vols. 1089

SMITH, Benjamin (d. 1852, of Ancaster). Farming diary, 1799-1849; account of his work and personal affairs as a settler and farmer in Upper Canada. MS, Public Archives, Toronto, 8 vols. 1090

SMITH, Mrs. Damaris Isabella (1831-1931). "Pioneer Wife," Farmer's Magazine, 1944. Autobiography of farm life in Ontario

in the mid-nineteenth century. Clippings in Hamilton Public
Library.   1091

SMITH, G. Watt. From the Plough to the Pulpit (Toronto,1947).
A boyhood in Scotland; training as a pastor of Free Church;
work in Glasgow; later, his ministry in Ottawa and Manitoba
churches.   1092

SMITH, Goldwin (1823-1910). Reminiscences (London, 1910). His
boyhood and education in England, at Eton and Oxford; educational work at Oxford and Manchester; his professorship at
Cornell;his life in Canada and reminiscences of public life
and politics in Canada.   1093

SMITH, Lieut. Col. Henry Robert. A Glimpse of the Past (Ottawa, 1912). Reminiscences of political life and events and
personalities in Quebec and Ottawa, by the sergeant-at-arms
of the Canadian parliament. A pamphlet in the University of
Toronto library.   1094

SMITH, Rev. James Frazer (b. 1858). Life's Waking Part (Toronto, 1937). Autobiography of a Canadian missionary; youth
in Canada; work in China and India.   1095

SMITH, Joseph E., of Philadelphia. Over There and Beck (New
York, 1918). An American's service with the Second Canadian
Division in France during World War I; St. Eloi, Somme, An-
cre, Arras.   1096

SMITH, Larratt William (1820-1905). Private diary, 1839-1905;
the private affairs and social life of a Toronto lawyer and
financier. MS, Toronto Public Libraries, 52 vols.   1097

SMITH, Captain Nicholas. Fifty-two Years at the Labrador Factory (London, 1937). Autobiography of a lifetime in Labrador and Newfoundland fisheries;a direct story of plain life
and work, with some adventures in fishing boats.   1098

SMITH, Thomas B. Backward Glances (Falifax, 1898). Contents
unknown. Since found to be history only.   1099

SMITH, William Edward (born 1864). A Canadian Doctor in West
China (Toronto, 1939). An autobiography of his childhood in
Canada; his work as a medical missionary in China.   1100

SMITH, Rev'd. William Stables. Perilous Adventures in Canada
(London, 1918). Career of a Scotch Presbyterian minister in
various parts of Canada, 1891-1896; God's mercy in a series

of remarkable escapes from violent deaths in every possible form.   1101

SNIDER, Charles Henry Jeremiah. Under the Red Jack (Toronto, 1928). Not seen. Since found to be history only.   1102

SNOW, Samuel. The Exile's Return (Cleveland, 1846). His part in the Canadian rebellion of 1838; trial and transportation; life in Tasmania; and return.   1103

SODEN, C. C. It's a Great Life (London, 1937). Autobiography of an adventurous life; including a section on his travels and odd jobs in Canada.   1104

SOMERVILLE, Alexander. Conservative Science of Nations (Montreal, 1860). A Canadian's experiences in economics and revolution in Europe and the British Isles; politics, agriculture, etc.   1105

SOUTHESK, James Carnegie, 9th Earl of (1827-1905). Travel diary, April 1859-February 1860; his tour through territories of the Hudson's Bay Company, hunting big and small animals. Saskatchewan and the Rocky Mountains (London, 1875).   1106

SPRINGETT, Mrs. Evelyn Cartier (Galt). For My Children's Children (Montreal, 1937). Autobiography of her family and social life in Quebec, after emigration from Kent; later life on prairie ranches in Alberta and Saskatchewan.   1107

SPROTT, Revd. John (1790-1869). Memorials, ed. G. W. Sprott (Edinburgh, 1906). It includes extracts from diaries, 1818-1869; life of a Scottish preacher in Nova Scotia; travels, sermons, parish work, personal affairs.   1108

SQUAIR, John. The Autobiography of a Teacher of French (Toronto, 1928). History of French teaching in Ontario; University of Toronto; only partly autobiographical.   1109

STAMER, William ("Mark Tapley"). Recollections of a Life of Adventure (London, 1866). Including a section on his travels and adventures in Canada.   1110

STANMORE, Arthur Charles Hamilton-Gordon, first baron (1829-1912). Wilderness Journeys in New Brunswick in 1862-1863 (St. John, 1864). Experiences of forest life, including excerpts from his journals; lieutenant-governor of New Brunswick.   1111

STANWELL-FLETCHER, Theodora C. Driftwood Valley (London, 1948) Reminiscences of two years spent in British Columbia, collecting wild life specimens with her husband for a Canadian museum; adventures in solitude. 1112

STEAD, James. Treasure Trek (London, 1936). Autobiography of travels and adventures: including a section on the Canadian wilds. 1113

STEELE, John Coucher (1817-1909). Reminiscences of a Pioneer (Simcoe County Pioneer and Hist. Soc., Pioneer Paper No. 4, Barrie, Ont., 1911). Pioneer life in Simcoe County, Ontario during the mid-nineteenth century. 1114

STEELE, Colonel S. B. (b. 1849). Forty Years in Canada (London, 1915). His boyhood in Simcoe County and Red River; his work in the North-West Mounted Police; frontier life and the advance of the frontier; military service in the Boer War and in the South African Police. 1115

STEPHENSON, Isaac (born 1829). Recollections of a Long Life (Chicago, 1915). Covering 1829-1915; his boyhood and early life in New Brunswick, with its local customs, social life, and lumbering industry; later, a political career in United States. 1116

STEWARD, Austin (b. 1794). Twenty-Two Years a Slave and Forty Years a Freeman (Rochester, N.Y., 1857). An autobiography of an American negro: including a long section, pp.183-290, on his experiences in Wilberforce Colony, Ontario. A copy in Toronto Public Libraries. 1117

STEWART, B. The Land of the Maple Leaf (London, 1908). Personal experiences in Manitoba and the west, as engineer on the Grand Trunk Pacific Railway; an unfavourable description of Canadian life and conditions. 1118

STEWART, Rt. Rev. Charles James, Bishop of Quebec. Missionary diaries, 1833-1837; travels and work in Ontario among settlers and Indians; preaching and S.P.G. work; extracts from diaries of various missionaries included. The Stewart Missions, ed. W. J. D. Waddilove (London, 1838). 1119

STEWART, Mrs. Frances (Browne) (1794-1872). Our Forest Home (Montreal, 1902). Autobiography of Irish settler in Canada, 1822-1872, at Peterborough, Ont.; social and domestic life of a cultured settler; made up from selections from letters and journals. 1120

STONE, C. Arnold (born 1852). Reminiscences; life in London, Ont.; founding of Canadian Kennel Club. MS, Toronto Public Libraries, 23 pp. (typewritten copy). 1121

STRACHAN, Rt. Rev. John (1778-1867). Visitation journal, August-October, 1828; visits of the first Bishop of Toronto to Anglican churches in Upper Canada. A travel journal; visits to missions on Lake Simcoe, and to Sault Ste. Marie and Michilimackinac; notes on Indian life and customs. Travel diary, 1846; visiting churches in the Niagara district and in southwest Upper Canada. MS, Public Archives, Toronto. Religious journal, July-October, 1842; a journey to the western portion of his diocese, with notes on early settlements and congregations. A Journal of Visitation (London, 1844). Extracts from his journals are included in, A.N.Bethune, Memoir of the Right Rev. John Strachan (Toronto, 1870). 1122

STRANG, Peter (1856-1934). Autobiography (Regina,1933); mimeographed His life as minister and superintendent of United Church of Canada's missions in southern Saskatchewan; personal affairs. Copy at University of Saskatchewan. 1123

STRANGE, Henry George Latimer;and STRANGE, Mrs.Kathleen (Redman). Never a Dull Moment (Toronto, 1941). Autobiography of Harry Strange, engineer and farmer; life in Klondyke and in Alberta; friendship with Jack London; his services in World War I. 1124

STRANGE, James (1753-1840). Fur-trading journal, 1785-1786; a record of a journey, from Bombay to Nootka Sound and Prince William's Sound; work in the maritime fur-trade. Journal and Narrative of the Commercial Expedition from Bombay (Madras, 1928). 1125

STRANGE, Mrs. Kathleen (Redman) (born 1896). With the West in Her Eyes (Toronto, 1937).Autobiography of life on an Alberta farm, from 1920; wheat farming, domestic and social life among settlers. 1126

STRAVAIGER (pseud. of Harry Mortimer Batten, b. 1888). Mountains of the Morning (Edinburgh, 1938). Emigration and life in Canada, the west and northern Ontario. 1127

STRICKLAND, Major Samuel (1809-1867). Twenty-Seven Years in Canada West (London, 1853) 2 vols. Experiences of an early settler in Huron territory, 1825-1851; work for the Canada Company and the government; travels, adventures, hunting; general conditions and prospects for emigrants. 1128

STUDLEY, J. T. Journal of a Sporting Nomad (London, 1912). A wanderer's life; including section on hunting in Canada and Newfoundland. 1129

STURGES-JONES, Marion. Babes in the Wood (New York, 1944). A light-hearted account of his boyhood and youth in Canada and the United States; World War I. 1130

SUTHERLAND, Thomas Jefferson. A Letter to Her Majesty, the British Queen (Albany, N.Y., 1841). An American's autobiographical narrative of service in the Canadian Rebellion of 1837; politics, military experiences, imprisonment; justification. Copy at Harvard. 1131

SUTTON, Francis (b. 1884). One-Arm Sutton (Toronto, 1930). An autobiography of travel and adventure; a sojourn in western Canada. 1132

SUTTON, George Miksch. Eskimo Year (New York, 1934). With walrus-hunting Eskimos in the Hudson's Bay region; igloo life; human relationships; adventures. 1133

SWALLOWS, Edward. Religious journal, 1848-1849; notes on Methodist life, work, and travel in Canada. Canadian Royal Soc. Trans. XXV (1931) Sec. II, 151-163. 1134

SYKES, Ella Constance. A Home Help in Canada (London, 1912). An author-traveller's investigation of conditions for emigrants; work as home help in western Canada; social, economic, domestic life in hotels and farm-houses. 1135

T., H. Private diary, 1838-1841; Canadian interest; contents unknown. MS, Ottawa Archives. 1136

TACHE, Mgr. Alexandre Antoine (b. 1823). Vingt Années de Missions dans le Nord-Ouest de l'Amérique (Montreal, 1866). A Catholic missionary's labors and travel in the Hudson's Bay and northwestern areas; later Archbishop of St. Boniface. Copy at Harvard and Bibliothèque St. Sulpice. 1137

TAIT, George. Autobiography (Halifax, N.S., 1878; 1892). Life of a deaf-mute, who first taught the deaf and dumb in Halifax. Copy in Dennis College, Acadia University. 1138

TALBOT, Edward Allen. Five Years' Residence in the Canadas (London, 1824) two vols. Experiences of and reflections on Canadian life, conditions, and customs, 1818-1823; government, education, towns, lives of settlers. 1139

TALMAN, James J. (ed.). Loyalist Narratives from Upper Canada (Champlain Soc.,XXVII, Toronto, 1947). A collection of diaries and personal reminiscences of United Empire Loyalists; Canadian travels, farming and settling, personal and family life, political affairs, loyalist motives, hardships of exiles and pioneers; interesting and valuable historical materials. Among the writers are: Richard Cartwright, Stephen Jarvis, Adam Crysler, Thomas Merritt, Henry Ruttan, Catherine White, Amelia Harris, James Dittrick. 1140

TAYLOR, Henry. Travel journal, August-November,1839; notes of a trip from Montreal to the eastern townships of Lower Canada. Journal of a Tour from Montreal (Quebec,1840). 1141

TEMPLE,D. Out with the Mounties (London, 1937). Personal narrative of service with the North-West Mounted Police. 1142

TEMPLE, Right Hon. Sir Richard (1826-1902). The Story of My Life (London, 1896) two vols. Autobiography of a statesman; includes a section on travel in Canada. 1143

THIBODO, Dr. Augustus J. (b. 1834?, of Kingston). Travel diary, June 1859-April 1860; from Ontario to Minnesota; then overland to Walla Walla; notes on natural history, places, people. Pacific Northwest Quar. XXXI (1940) 287-347. 1144

THOMAS, Benjamin. Religious note-book, 1818; work of Baptist in Canada. MS, McMaster University, 210 pp. 1145

THOMAS, C. The Frontier Schoolmaster (Montreal, 1880). Autobiography of teaching, farming, political, military life in Quebec Province; interesting. 1146

THOMAS, F. Travel journal, 1833; an emigrant from London to Quebec; shipwreck near Cape Ray. MS, Ottawa Archives. 1147

THOMAS, Sir William Beach. The Way of a Countryman (London, 1944). Includes a section on travel and journalism in Canada. 1148

THOMPSON, C. W. Life is a Jest (London, 1924). Autobiography of a traveller; testimony of a wanderer on social life and conditions in Canada. 1149

THOMPSON, George S.(b.1848). Up to Date (Peterboro 1885).Life as a lumberjack in Ontario from 1870; vicissitudes and successes in confessional style; interesting. Copy in Victoria College, Toronto. 1150

THOMPSON, J. R. Private diary, 1837; notes on the effects of the 1837 rebellion in a back township in Upper Canada. Canadian Hist. Rev. XI (1930), 223-232. 1151

THOMPSON, Sergeant James (1732-1830). Military diaries, 1759; 1775-1776; 1779-1781; 1787-1788; the first gives details of the siege of Quebec;the others were kept while he was overseer of works at Quebec; with memoranda relating to buildings, engineering, upkeep, and some weather notes. MS, Literary and Historical Society of Quebec; photostat in Ottawa Archives. Extracts in: Lit. Hist. Soc. Quebec Trans. No. 22 (1898) 57-62; Lit. Hist. Soc. Quebec Hist. Docs., 7th Ser. (1905). 1152

THOMPSON, John. Private journal, 1798; contents unknown. MS, photograph, Alberta Provincial Library, Edmonton. 1153

THOMPSON, Samuel (1810-1886). Reminiscences of a Canadian Pioneer for the Last Fifty Years (Toronto, 1884). Emigration to Canada in 1833; life in the backwoods and in Toronto and Quebec; work as a journalist; politics, the rebellion,business, public life and persons, British-American League,etc. Partly printed in Rose-Belford's Canadian Monthly, Vol. VII (1881). 1154

THOMSON, Captain John (1787-1870). Private diary, 1821-1838; voyage from Leith to Upper Canada; experiences of a settler at Orillia, Ontario; farming; the 1837 rebellion. MS, Public Archives, Toronto. Selections published in the Orillia Packet and Times, and published in pamphlet form; Extracts from the Diary of Captain John Thomson, edited James Talman (Orillia, 1932). Copy in University of Toronto. 1155

THORNHILL, Mary Elizabeth (b. 1865). Between Friends (Toronto 1935).Reminiscences of her family life and public events in Toronto; schools, social life, sports, celebrities; travels in Europe; a pleasant record. 1156

THORNTON, Major John. Travel journal, June-October 1849; from New York to Niagara and through Upper Canada; hotels,parks, trains, towns, general conditions. Diary of a Tour (London, 1850). 1157

TOD, John. Fur-trading journal,1841-1843; details of his work and life in the fur-trade;at Thompson's River Fort. MS,Provincial Library, Victoria. 1158

TODD, A. Hamlyn. Private diary, March-July, 1885; experiences of an officer of the Guards Company of Sharpshooters of Ottawa during the Saskatchewan rebellion. MS, University of Saskatchewan. 1159

[TODD, Henry Cook (died 1862)]. Items in the Life of an Usher (Quebec, 1855). An autobiography of a man who came to Canada in 1832; a hodgepodge of anecdotes and information on a wide range of subjects. Copy in Toronto Public Libraries. 1160

TOLFREY, Frederic. The Sportsman in Canada (London, 1845), two vols. He arrived in Quebec in 1816; fishing on Jacques Cartier River, hunting, social life at an army post in Quebec; impoverishment and life as farmer and labourer. 1161

TOLLEMACHE, Hon. Stanley. Reminiscences of the Yukon (London, 1912). His varied experiences, 1898-1909; mining, trapping, trading, prospecting; pioneering and frontier life at Dawson and Pelly River. 1162

TOLMIE, Dr. William Fraser (1812-1888). Fur-trading journal, 1833-1836; a doctor with the Hudson's Bay Company; beginning at Nisqually House and ending at Fort Vancouver; excellent descriptions of life at the forts, Indians, botanical material, etc. MS, Provincial Library, Victoria, 135 pp. (typewritten copy); see, Washington Hist. Quar. III (1912), 229-241. 1163

TOMISON, William; and COCKING, Matthew. Fur-trading journals, 1776-1777; journeys between York Fort and Cumberland House in service of Hudson's Bay Company. MS, photostat, University of Toronto Library, 22 pp. 1164

TRAILL, Mrs. Catherine Parr (1802-1899). Backwoods of Canada (London, 1836). Experiences of the wife of an emigrant officer; her three years in various parts of Canada; a woman's advice to emigrants on domestic affairs. 1165

TRELAWNEY-ANSELL, Edward Clarence. I Followed Gold (London, 1938). An Englishman's travels and adventures in search of gold; includes sections in Canada and Alaska. 1166

TREMBLAY, Alfred. Cruise of the Minnie Maud (Quebec, 1921). His experiences in Arctic seas and Hudson's Bay, 1910-1913; personal affairs and scientific details on mineral deposits and natural history. 1167

TROTTER, Beecham. *A Horseman and the West* (Toronto, 1925). An autobiography of early life in the Canadian west; farming in Manitoba in the eighties; horse-ranching; pioneer life; and the opening of the west.   1168

THROUGHTON, F. J. *A Bachelor's Paradise* (London, 1931). A life on the Canadian prairies in the eighties.   1169

TRUDEAU, Romuald (1802-1888). "Mes Tablettes, 1820-1850;" a French-Canadian pharmacist in Montreal; president of the St. Jean Baptiste Society; public happenings in Quebec Province; important for details of the 1837 rebellion in Canada. *MS, Bibliothèque St. Sulpice*, Montreal, 13 books.   1170

TUPPER, Sir Charles (1821-1915). *Recollections of Sixty Years* (London, 1914); *Political Reminiscences*, ed. by W.A. Harkin (London, 1914). Memories of politics in Nova Scotia, 1864-1900; the Canadian Pacific Railway; Federation in Canada; development of national policy; imperial relations; opinion and memories of Canadian statesmen and events.   1171

TURGEON, Hon. Onésiphore. *Un Tribut à la Race Acadienne* (Montreal, 1928). Memoirs of a New Brunswick senator, 1871-1927; a detailed record of political, agricultural, economic, and educational matters. Copy in Bibliothèque St. Sulpice. 1172

TURNER, C. E. *A Parson across the Rockies* (London, 1927). Apparently missionary in Canada; mostly about churches. 1173

TURNOR, Philip (1752?-1800?). Travel journal, September 1778 - August 1792; Northern Canada west of Hudson's Bay. *Journals of Samuel Hearne and Philip Turnor*, ed. J. B. Tyrrell (Toronto, 1934), 195-491, 557-577.   1174

TYRER, Alfred Henry (1870-1942). *And a New Earth* (Toronto, 1941). Autobiography of an English-born schoolteacher, advocate of birth control and minister, who spent part of his life in Muskoka district, Ontario.   1175

TYRRELL, Mrs. Mary Edith (née Carey) (1870?-1945). *I Was There* (Toronto, 1938). An autobiography of the wife of the famous geologist and explorer; including life in Ottawa and in the Klondyke; domestic and family life; a woman's view of the excitements and life of the gold-fields.   1176

UMFREVILLE, Edward. Travel journal, June-July, 1784; by canoe from Pais Plat on Lake Superior to Portage de l'Isle in the

Rivière Ouinipigne; topography; fur-trading. MS, Provincial Library, Victoria; University of Toronto, etc. (copy). 1177

UNWIN, Charles (1829-1918). Autobiographical Sketch (Toronto, 1910). Brief account of boyhood in England, and reminiscences of early days in Toronto. 1178

VALE, Edmund. Straw into Gold (London, 1939). A journalist's life of travel; including section on Canada. 1179

VANCOUVER, Captain George (1758-1798). Exploration journals, April 1791-October 1795; journey around the world; exploration in the Pacific north-west; Puget Sound and north-west coast; scientific and official report. Voyage of Discovery to the North Pacific Ocean (London, 1798) 3 vols. 1180

VAN DYKE, Prof. John C. The Open Spaces (London, 1922). Reminiscences of boyhood on northwestern ranches; cattle business cowboys, Indians; travels, hunting, primitive scene. 1181

VAN KOUGHNET, Lieut. Edmund Barker (1849-1905). Nautical diary, June 1884-April 1885; a Toronto man's narrative of his service in the Nile expedition. Lady Jane Van Koughnet, The Van Gochnats (London, 1910) 17-93. 1182

VAN VLIET, Traver. Diary, early 19th Century; records of early settlement in Quebec; pioneer life, family affairs, travel between Lacolle and Montreal; the 1837 rebellion, etc. Canadian Hist. Rev. XI (1930) 38-48. 1183

VARDON, Roger. English Bloods (Ottawa, 1930). A young Englishman learning to farm in the Muskoka district; humourous account of hard work and difficulties. Copy at Harvard. 1184

VERCHÈRES DE BOUCHERVILLE, René Thomas. A Merchant's Clerk in Upper Canada, trans. W. S. Wallace (Toronto, 1935). A short autobiography of his experiences in Ontario and of his work for the North-West Company, 1804-1811. 1185

VERREAU, Zephirin (1871-1891). Vie de Zephirin Verreau (Quebec, 1894). Biography of a devout French-Canadian Catholic who was a pupil at the Seminaire de Rimouski; it includes extracts from his pious journals. 1186

VETCH, Governor Samuel (1668-1732). Sea journal, July-October 1711; expedition from Boston to Quebec in the fleet commanded by Sir Hovenden Walker. Nova Scotia Hist. Soc. Colls IV (1884) 105-110. 1187

VIDAL, Lois. __Magpie__ (New York, 1934). An Englishwoman's life of travel and odd jobs; Canadian section. 1188

VIETH, Lieut.Frederick Harris D. __Recollections of the Crimean Campaign__ (Montreal, 1907). A Canadian's service in the Crimean War; military service and social life; the later section records his sporting life and adventures in a garrison in Lower Canada, 1853-1866. 1189

VIGER, Jacques (1787-1858). Military journal, 1813; movements while serving as captain in the Voltigeurs; Sackett's Harbour. Extracts in, "Lettres de Jacques Viger," __Revue Canadienne__, 1914. 1190

VILLIERS, Hon. Katharine. __Memoirs of a Maid of Honour__ (London 1931). Includes travels and society life in Canada in 1913-1914 with the Duke of Connaught, Governor-General. 1191

VITRY, Père. Religious journal, 1738-1740; notes of a Jesuit serving as almoner to French troops fighting the Tchikachas Indians. __Nova Francia__, IV (1929) 146-166. 1192

VON GRAFFENRIED, Friedrich (b. 1792). __Sechs Jahre in Canada, 1813-1819__ (Bern, 1891); republished from __Jahresbericht der Geographischen Gesellschaft von Bern__, Vol. X. An account, partly in diary form, of a journey to Canada with De Meuron regiment and of experience in Lord Selkirk's Red River Settlement. 1193

VOYER, Ludger Napoleon (1842-1876, of Quebec). Private diary, 1860-1872; work as superintendent of police in Quebec Province; travels in Europe; comments on French-Canadian public life and its celebrities. A.N. Montpetit, __Major L. N. Voyer__ (Quebec, 1876), passim. 1194

WACKET, Corporal E. "Experiences with the First Western Ontario Regiment," __Waterloo Hist. Soc.__, __5th Annual Rep.__ (1917). Service with the Canadian forces in France during World War I; Ypres, etc. 1195

WALDEN, Arthur Treadwell (1871?-1948). __A Dog-Puncher on the Yukon__ (Montreal, 1928). Experiences of freighting with dogs in the Yukon River and Klondyke areas, 1896-1902. 1196

WALDRON, Samuel J. __Reminiscences of My Life__ (Victoria, 1938). Not seen. 1197

WALFORD, Thomas. Travel journal, 1768-1769; voyage on behalf of the Royal Society to Churchill River, Hudson's Bay, and thirteen months' residence there; return journey; scientific interest. Archaeologia, XIII (1770). 1198

WALKER, Alexander. Hours off and on Sentry (Montreal, 1859). Personal narrative of military career and adventures; partly in Canada. 1199

WALKER, Annie L. Leaves from the Canadian Backwoods (Montreal 1861). Not seen. Since found to be poetry. 1200

WALKER, Sir Hovenden (1656?-1728). Naval journal, April-October, 1711; expedition from Boston to Quebec; a record and a justification of the disastrous expedition for which he was cashiered from the navy. A Journal or Full Account of the Late Expedition (London, 1720). 1201

WALKER, James H. A Scotsman in Canada (London, 1935). Travels and various jobs of an emigrant in Western Canada; Canadian social conditions; a lively account. 1202

WALKER, William Wesley (b. 1858). By Northern Lakes (Toronto, 1896). Reminiscences of missionary work and travel in Ontario; hunting; character sketches. 1203

WALLACE, Archer (b.1884). I Believe in People (Toronto,1936). Religious life in Canada. Not autobiography. 1204

WALLACE, Sir Donald Mackenzie (1841-1919). The Web of Empire (London, 1902). Official diary of the tour of the Duke and Duchess of Cornwall and York, 1901; public occasions, speeches, celebrities. 1205

WALLACE, W. B. "Six Years in a Juvenile Court," University Mag., XVI (1917), 362-378. Personal reminiscences of crime and delinquency in Canada. 1206

[WARBURTON, George Drought (1816-1857)]. Hochelaga; or England in the New World (London, 1846) 2 vols. Military services in Upper and Lower Canada; impressions; copy in Toronto Public Libraries. 1207

WARE, Titus Hibbert (1810-1890). Travel diary, July-November, 1844; a lawyer's visit to Orillia, Ontario; notes on land, society, roads, settlers; accounts. MS, Toronto Public Libraries. 1208

WASHBURN, Stanley (b.1878). Trails, Trappers, and Tender-feet (London, 1913). Expeditions in the Canadian Rockies. 1209

WATSON, John Cameron. One Man's Furrow (London, 1940). Autobiography; includes section on farming in Canada. 1210

WATSON, Robert. A Boy of the Great North-West (Ottawa, 1930). His boyhood in British Columbia; schooling, hunting, fishing; Indians and their customs; winter in Manitoba; rebellion of 1870. Copy in Bibliothèque St. Sulpice. 1211

WATSON, William Ritchie (b.1904). My Desire (Edmonton, 1932); I Give You Yesterday (Toronto, 1938). The first is a brief, the second is a longer autobiography of a man never able to use his arms, who uses his feet to perform the functions of hands; Helen Keller type of successful struggle to overcome physical handicaps and to become socially integrated. 1212

WEBLING, Peggy. Peggy (London, 1924). An actress's autobiography; includes theatrical tours in Canada. 1213

WEBSTER, Rev. John. Methodist diary, June 1871-April 1872; a record of missionary travel and preaching in Ontario;Muskoka district. MS, Victoria College, Toronto, Archives Dept., Pam. T. 123, We. 1214

WEBSTER, John Clarence (b. 1863). Those Crowded Years (Shediac, N.B., 1944). The career of a Shediac physician, 1863 to 1944; his friends and his work as an antiquary and historian in New Brunswick. Copy at Harvard. 1215

WEBSTER, Mrs. Susanna (1817-1905). Reminiscences of her emigration as a child and settlement at London Township, 1819-1821; followed by reminiscences of her son-in-law, A.Screaton. MS, Toronto Public Libraries, 9 pp. 1216

WEIR, William (1823-1905). Sixty Years in Canada (Montreal, 1903).His early life in Scotland and in Montreal from 1837; Canadian politics,tariff movement, silver coinage, banking, and real estate speculation. 1217

WELLS, Kenneth McNeill. The Owl Pen (Toronto, 1947). Newspaperman and his artist wife living in a log-cabin in Medante township, Ontario; trials and tribulations of living in the wilderness. 1218

WELSH, Norbert (born 1845). The Last Buffalo Hunter: by Mary Weekes (New York, 1939). A dictated autobiography of an old hunter and Indian-trader; fur-trading and hunting in Saskatchewan; farming; Northwest Rebellion. 1219

WEST, Edward. Homesteading (London, 1918). Experiences of a settler on the Saskatchewan prairie during his first years; locating homestead, breaking the prairie, farming. 1220

WEST, George T.(1824-1896). Private diary, 1861-1896; emigration from England; trading in the Indian Ocean; his life on farm at Mountain Lake, near Minden, Ont.,from 1865 to 1896. MS, Toronto Public Libraries, 6 vols. 1221

WEST, Rev.John (1778-1845). Religious and missionary journal, May 1820-October 1823; from England to Winnipeg; his labors as chaplain for the Hudson's Bay Company at Red River colony; missionaries, Indians, settlers; return. The Substance of a Journal (London,1824); reprinted (Montreal, 1866).1222

WESTBURY,G.H. Misadventures of a Working Hobo in Canada (London, 1930). A disenchanted narrative of working-class life among settlers in Canada; his work as a farming inspector; Ontario and Toronto. 1223

WESTON, Thomas Chesmer (born 1832, of Ottawa). Reminiscences among the Rocks in Canada (Toronto, 1899). Memories of exploration and geological work; with the Canadian Geological Survey in Nova Scotia and Quebec; travel and sport. 1224

WHITE, Mrs. Henry. "Reminiscences," Ontario Hist. Soc.Papers VII (1906) 153-157. Memories of pioneer settlers in Cobourg in Upper Canada. 1225

WHITE, John (d. 1800). Travel diary, June 1792-April 1794; a politician's journey from Montreal to Kingston; happenings there until election to House of Assembly; his life at Niagara. MS, Toronto Public Libraries, Robertson Coll. (typed copy). 1226

WHITTAKER, Charles Edward (born 1864). Arctic Eskimo (London, 1937). An autobiography of fifty years work and observation among Eskimos in the Canadian far north. 1227

WICKERSHAM, J. Old Yukon: Tales, Trails, and Trials (Washington, 1938). American; about Alaska. 1228

WIEDEMANN, Thomas. Cheechako into Sourdough (Portland, Oregon 1942). Autobiography of the "Klondike Kid." 1229

WILLIAMS, Sir Ralph. How I Became a Governor (London, 1913). Miscellaneous experience of working for the British government; it includes sections on his governorship in Newfoundland. 1230

WILLIAMS, Revd. Thomas (1810-1899). "Memories of a Pioneer," Simcoe County Pioneer and Hist. Soc. Pioneer Papers (1917). Memories of Methodist missionary work and travel in Ontario in the early nineteenth century. 1231

WILLIAMS, W. H. Travel diary, July-December, 1881; a journalist's trip from Toronto to the Rocky Mountains in the party of Lord Lorne, the Governor-General. Manitoba and the Northwest (Toronto, 1882). 1232

WILLISON, Sir John Stephen (1856-1927).Reminiscences, Political and Personal (Toronto, 1919). Canadian journalism and politics, from 1872; Ontario parliament and press gallery; The Globe; Liberal politicians. First published in Canadian Magazine, 1918. 1233

WILLSON, Henry Beckles (1869-1942). From Quebec to Piccadilly (London, 1929). Autobiography of a Canadian-born journalist and author who passed much of his life in England; Liberal politics from 1900; World War I; Canadian-British relations and memories. 1234

WILSON, Sir Charles Rivers (1831-1916).Chapters from My Official Life (London, 1916). Includes a section on his work on railroads in Canada, 1894-1909. 1235

WILSON, Edward F. Missionary Work among the Ojebway Indians (London, 1886). Religious work and travel among Indians in Ontario, at Sarnia, Garden River, and Algoma; trip to London with chiefs and visit with Prince of Wales. 1236

WILSON, James (1777-1851?). Religious diary, May-July, 1817; a Methodist's journey from Dublin to Quebec. Narrative of a Voyage (Dublin, 1822). 1237

WINSLOW, Joshua (1727-1801).Military journal, March-December, 1750; with Lawrence on two expeditions to Chignecto, N. B.; naval and military movements. The Journal of Joshua Winslow (New Brunswick Museum, 1936). 1238

WITHERSPOON, John, of Annapolis, N.S. Prison diary, November 1757-September 1759; captured by French and imprisonment at Quebec, narrative of the siege; his hardships and religious difficulties. Nova Scotia Hist. Soc. Colls. II (1879-1880) 31-62. 1239

WIX, Rev. Edward, of St. John's. Missionary journal, February-August, 1835; work and travels in Newfoundland; life of the Indians; social life; a pleasant record. Six Months of a Newfoundland Missionary's Journal (London, 1836). 1240

WOLFE, Major-General James (1727-1759). Military journal, May-August, 1759; military details of British expedition against Quebec; maneuvers and skirmishes; staff matters relating to the siege. MS, McCord Museum, Montreal; photostats in New York Public Library and McGill University. 1241

WOLSELEY, Garner Joseph, 1st Viscount (1833-1913). The Story of a Soldier's life (London, 1903) 2 vols. Includes section on his military service in Canada. 1242

WOOD, Colonel J. H. War journal, 1812; extracts dealing with military affairs during the war of 1812. Women's Canadian Hist. Soc. Toronto Trans. No. 5 (1905). 1243

WOOD, James. The Adventures, Sufferings, and Observations of James Wood (London, 1840). His emigration to Canada in 1836; travels and experiences among settlers, in Newfoundland and New Brunswick; account of their and his miseries, and warnings to emigrants. Pamphlet, Ottawa Archives. 1244

WOODINGTON, Henry. Prison diary, 1869-1870; notes of a prisoner in Fort Garry during the Red River rebellion. Niagara Hist. Soc. Proc. XXV (1913) 32-55. 1245

WOODSWORTH, Rev. James (d. 1917). Thirty Years in the Canadian North-West (Toronto, 1917). His Methodist circuit work in Saskatchewan, Alberta, and British Columbia, from 1868; Indians and settlers. 1246

WOON, Basil. Eyes West (London, 1940). A wanderer's autobiography; including emigration as boy to Canada; with surveying party to the Pacific; and in the gold-rush. 1247

WORBY, John (b. 1911). The Other Half (London, 1937). Unsavory life of a hobo and a spiv; including experiences in the United States and Canada. 1248

WORK, John (1792-1861). Fur-trading journals, 1823-1835; his labours for the Hudson's Bay Company during the peak of the north-western fur-trade; life and trade and travels; Columbia River, York Factory, Astoria, Fort George, Fraser River, Snake River, Fort Vancouver, etc. See, Canadian Hist. Assoc. Annual Report (1929), 21-29; Washington Hist. Quar.

III (1912), V (1914), VI (1915); Oregon Hist. Soc. Quar. X (1909), XIII (1912), XIV (1913), XXIV (1923).The Journal of John Work, edited W. S. Lewis and P.C. Phillips (Cleveland, 1923). Several MSS, Provincial Library, Victoria. 1249

WORTHINGTON. Dr. E. D. (died 1895). Reminiscences of Student Life and Practice (Sherbrooke, Quebec, 1897). Medical study in Quebec; service in the 1837 rebellion; his teaching and practice of medicine in Edinburgh and Quebec. 1250

WRENCH, John Evelyn. Immortal Years (London, 1944). Service as relations officer in Canada during World War II. 1251

WRIGHT, C. M. (d. 1918). War diary, 1917; notes of a Canadian soldier during 1st World War; with the 14th Brigade on the Western Front. Ontario Hist. Soc. Papers XXIII (1926), 511-522. 1252

WRIGHT, Stephen S.Narrative and Recollections of Van Dieman's Land (New York,18?). An American's service in the Canadian rebellion; capture and transportation;his life among aborigines and convicts in Tasmania.Copy in University of Toronto Library. 1253

WRIGHT, William Elliott (1785-1869). "Biography and Extracts from the Diary," Women's Canadian Hist. Soc. Toronto Trans. XIII (1914), 25-37. Notes of a naval officer who settled in Upper Canada. 1254

YATES, Robert L. When I Was a Harvester (Toronto, 1930).Boy's experiences harvesting in the Canadian northwest. 1255

ANON. A Year in Manitoba (Edinburgh, 1882): and a sequel, The Colonist at Home Again (London, 1889). Experiences of a retired officer settling his sons in Canada,1880; his life in Manitoba; return to England; views on emigration. 1256

YOUMANS, Letitia. Campaign Echoes (Toronto, 1893). Early life in Ontario; but mostly her life and work as a leader of the temperance movement in Canada. 1257

YOUNG, Rev. Arminius. A Methodist Missionary in Labrador (Toronto, 1916). Missionary work and camp life at Komotik, Mud Hole, and Grand Lake,1903-1905; fight against intemperance; the first missionaries in the area. 1258

YOUNG, The Rev. Egerton Ryerson (1840-1909). By Canoe and Dog-Train (London, 1890); On the Indian Trail (London, 1897);

Stories from Indian Wigwams and Northern Campfires (London, 1897); The Battle of the Bears (London, 1907). Reminiscences of incidents in the life of a missionary among the Cree and Salteaux Indians in the Georgian Bay region, during the sixties to the eighties; adventure and romance. 1259

YOUNG, Sir Frederick (1817-1913). A Pioneer of Imperial Federation in Canada (London, 1902). Thirty years' work for imperial federation; his travels and propaganda. "A Few Random Recollections of Certain Incidents of My Life,: MS, The Royal Empire Society, London, No. 107626, 85 pp. 1260

YOUNG, Rev. George (1821-1910, of Pictou). Manitoba Memories (Toronto, 1897). Methodist's educational and religious work in the Red River settlement,1868 to 1884; politics; the rebellion. 1261

YOUNG, J. Peat. A Newcomer in Canada (London, 1924). Farming and pioneer life in Saskatchewan; social life and friendships; advice to emigrants. 1262

ZOLO, Serge. Sentenced to Adventure (London, 1936). Journalist in Canada; his three years in the Arctic; driving dog-teams; work in the Alberta Police; also smuggling and rum-running over the border. 1263

ADDENDA

ANON. Fur-trader's journal, October 1799-April 1800; kept by a trader in charge of Rocky Mountain Fort. Washington Hist. Quar. XIX (1928). 1264

ARGALL, Phyllis (b. 1909). My Life with the Enemy (New York, 1944). A Canadian-born woman's life in Japan, with account of imprisonment during World War II. 1265

BROWN, Eddie. Road Pirate (London, 1934). Confessions of English motor bandit; including Canadian experiences. 1266

CHAMBERS, William Nesbitt. Yoljuluk (London,1929).Autobiography of Canadian missionary in Asiatic Turkey from 1879; his work among the Kurds; Turkish wars. 1267

COLEMAN, Arthur Philemon (1852-1939, geologist). The Canadian Rockies (London, 1911). His experiences travelling and exploring in the Canadian Rockies, 1884-1908. 1268

DE CHARLEVOIX, Pierre François Xavier (1682-1761). Travel diary, June 1720-January 1723; adventures in Canada and the Illinois country; Indians. Journal d'un Voyage (Paris 1744) and several later editions. 1269

DE DIÉREVILLE, N. (b.1670?). Relation du Voyage du Port Royal (Rouen,1708); trans. as Relation of the Voyage to Port Royal (Toronto, 1933). His experiences during a trading expedition to Acadia; Indian life. 1270

DIXON, Capt.Charles C. A Million Miles in Sail; by John H.McCulloch (London, 1934). Lively autobiography of a Nova Scotian sailor; life on Nova Scotia seaboard; in clipper ships and later under steam; service in World War I. 1271

GRAHAM,E.Maud. A Canadian Girl in South Africa (Toronto,1905) Journey and a year's teaching in concentration camp schools in South Africa; her experiences and observations. 1272

GREY, F. W. Seeking Fortune in America (London, 1912). At the Guelf Agricultural College, 1890; training and farm work in Canada; odd jobs there and in U.S.A. 1273

HERKLOTS, Rev. H. G. G. The First Winter (London,1935). English clergyman settled in Winnipeg; narrative of early experiences on prairie and in the bush; candid. 1274

McCLURE, Samuel (b. 1857). My Autobiography (London, 1914).An Irishman raised in Argentina and Quebec;odd chores and jobs of an immigrant in Canada;writing, journalism, and publishing of McClure's Magazine. 1275

MORGAN-POWELL, S. Memories That Live (London,1930).Canadian's lively reminiscences of world travel and of the theater and actors and actresses in England and France. 1276

INDEX

This index covers only the broad matters and main emphases of the diaries and autobiographies. Since these documents cover so many matters, no attempt has been made to index all the minor topics which are reported in the bibliography itself. The only way to gather all the material on any topic is to search through the bibliography itself, the index being intended only as a guide to the chief documents on the subjects listed. The references are to the numbers given after each item in the list.

ACADIA, 123, 225, 347, 591, 860, 1270.

ADVENTUROUS LIVES, 219, 286, 581, 761, 870, 872, 949, 1001, 1104, 1110, 1132, 1140.

ALBERTA, see under: North-West Mounted, Politics, Religious Settlers, Social, Travel.

AMERICAN REVOLUTION, see under Military.

ANGLICANISM, see under Religious.

ARCHITECTURE, see Arts.

ARCTIC EXPLORATION, 90, 133, 147, 158, 238, 267, 304, 418 466, 523, 541, 556, 613, 645 652, 750, 756, 765, 800, 902 975, 992, 1075, 1084, 1167.

ARTS (including architecture, bookselling, music, painting, radio), 9, 81, 175, 357 425, 584, 598, 633, 660, 760 785, 786, 789, 807, 891, 1057, 1213, 1276. See also, Journalism; Writers.

BAPTISTS, see under Religious.

BOER WAR, see under Military.

BOOKSELLING, see Arts.

BRITISH COLUMBIA, see under Politics, Religious, Settlers, Social, Travel.

CATHOLICISM, see under Religious.

CLIMBING, see under Sport.

COMMERCE, 174, 232, 342, 359, 389, 450, 467, 558, 684, 718 725, 743, 782, 857, 896, 937 938, 1088, 1097, 1116, 1128 1171, 1185, 1217, 1270.

CONSERVATION, 470.

CRIME, 242, 462, 878, 1030, 1206, 1248, 1263, 1266. See also, North-West Mounted; Police.

DOMESTIC LIFE, 214, 217, 381. See also, Social.

EDUCATION, 94, 96, 119, 221, 297, 314, 389, 471, 501, 574 578, 608, 619, 657, 674, 678 718, 738, 746, 762, 766, 783 799, 801, 857, 864, 940, 970 1016, 1026, 1031, 1033, 1093 1109, 1146, 1160, 1175, 1211 1250, 1272.

EMIGRANTS, 1, 101, 252, 454, 579, 643, 904, 997, 1106, 1139, 1165, 1202. See also, Settlers.

ENGINEERING, 788. See also, Railways.

ESKIMO LIFE, 1013, 1133, 1227

INDEX

See also, Arctic Exploration Travel (Arctic).

FENIANS, 199, 390, 596, 724, 1024, 1063.

FIRE BRIGADE, 787.

FISHING, see Sport.

FREE CHURCH, see under Religious.

FRENCH AND INDIAN WARS, see under Military.

FUR TRADE:
General, 83, 203, 273, 414 516, 561, 583, 707, 751, 752 771, 797, 876, 883, 1125, 1158, 1177, 1219, 1264.
Hudson's Bay Company. Before 1800: 56, 264, 563, 621 636, 654, 946, 1009, 1164. From 1800 to 1849: 16, 59, 60, 205, 210, 316, 393, 457 536, 669, 735, 741, 772, 775 778, 902, 1074, 1163, 1222. 1249. From 1850 to 1900: 25 69, 70, 71, 122, 191, 211, 282, 283, 475, 479, 515, 557 755, 780, 810, 815, 839, 1004. Twentieth Century: 204 720, 1020.
North-West Company, 202, 284, 405, 437, 537, 562, 740 744, 758, 773, 796, 1185.

GOLDRUSH, Klondike and Yukon, 14, 79, 86, 128, 146, 312, 354, 483, 546, 552, 649, 714 734, 838, 872, 924, 1056, 1124, 1162, 1176, 1229, 1247

GOVERNORS-GENERAL, 185, 827. See also, Society.

HUDSON'S BAY, see, Arctic, Fur Trade.

HUNTING, see Sport.

INDIAN CAPTIVES, 382, 490, 622

INDIAN LIFE AND AFFAIRS, 22, 27, 64, 168, 187, 255, 278, 444, 491, 505, 525, 613, 629 633, 707, 747, 944, 1007. Material on these topics is common in many other documents, especially in those listed under Fur-Trade, Military, Religious.

JOURNALISM, 140, 149, 164, 180 188, 239, 291, 292, 332, 366 507, 514, 526, 540, 542, 640 700, 763, 768, 786, 959, 1017, 1148, 1154, 1179, 1218 1232, 1233, 1234, 1263, 1275 See also, Writers.

KLONDIKE, see Gold-Rush.

LABRADOR, 634, 993, 1002, 1098 See also under, Religious, Settlers, Travel.

LAW PRACTICE, 105, 157, 206, 376, 511, 708, 806, 933, 958 967, 1026, 1097.

LIGHTHOUSES, 664, 987.

LOUISBOURG, Siege of, see under Military.

LOYALISTS, 93, 118, 228, 445, 617, 719, 1140.

MANITOBA, see under North-West Mounted, Politics, Ranching Religious, Social.

MEDICAL, 108, 177, 258, 280, 296, 362, 502, 511, 557, 565 589, 600, 607, 645, 671, 756 799, 834, 851, 920, 990, 1033, 1082, 1100, 1163, 1170 1212, 1215, 1250.

METHODISTS, see under Religious.

MILITARY:
General, including garrison duty and minor wars, 12 92, 100, 154, 156, 190, 308

INDEX

310, 317, 333, 334, 353, 355, 373, 374, 394, 419, 476, 506, 510, 522, 599, 618, 681, 690, 762, 811, 845, 868, 875, 887, 895, 899, 906, 933, 978, 991, 1024, 1087, 1146, 1161, 1189, 1192, 1199, 1207, 1242.

French and Indian Wars, including sieges of Louisbourg and Quebec, 7, 19, 20, 29, 30-34, 36-49, 51-53, 88, 163, 303, 320, 321, 327, 329, 330, 333, 336, 345, 348, 353, 436, 453, 463, 485, 487, 568, 655, 676, 757, 774, 795, 844, 847, 877, 918, 955, 1018, 1238, 1239, 1241.

American Revolution, 50, 51, 52, 53, 54, 91, 193, 216, 331, 337, 353, 380, 417, 427, 528, 594, 697, 719, 819, 847, 932, 1028, 1041, 1070, 1152. See also, Loyalists.

War of 1812, 58, 82, 189, 196, 294, 375, 416, 450, 518, 824, 882, 989, 996, 1243.

Rebellion of 1837, including narratives of political exiles, 61, 62, 82, 162, 180, 368, 376, 385, 420, 458, 467, 593, 661, 689, 695, 710, 716, 804, 833, 848, 956, 962, 991, 1012, 1080, 1103, 1131, 1151, 1155, 1170, 1183, 1250, 1253.

North-West Rebellions, 72, 106, 166, 199, 305, 334, 385, 486, 508, 564, 640, 1159, 1211, 1245.

Boer War, 183, 335, 543, 701, 767, 863, 977, 1033, 1115.

World War I, 11, 102, 115, 127, 144, 198, 220, 251, 261, 298, 300, 346, 355, 361, 448, 462, 464, 498, 544, 642, 644, 667, 723, 726, 737, 746, 799, 820, 842, 846, 880, 890, 898, 931, 949, 969, 973, 977, 1013, 1033, 1048, 1049, 1073, 1096, 1124, 1130, 1195, 1252.

World War II, 138, 257, 798, 1227, 1265.

MINING AND PROSPECTING, 107, 371, 549, 625, 705, 769, 809, 840, 927, 1002, 1166. See also, Gold-Rush.

MISSIONARIES, see Religious.

MORAVIANS, see under Religious.

MUSIC, see Arts.

NAVAL, 120, 215, 259, 345, 818, 941, 1003, 1036, 1182, 1187, 1201. See also, Seamen.

NAVAL EXPLORATION, 55, 328, 465, 547, 821, 968, 1180. See Voyages.

NEW BRUNSWICK, see under Politics, Religious, Settlers, Social, Travel.

NEWFOUNDLAND, see under Politics, Religious, Settlers, Social, Travel.

NORTH-WEST COMPANY, see under Fur-Trade.

NORTH-WEST MOUNTED POLICE, 209, 212, 306, 315, 351, 356, 378, 422, 434, 601, 683, 843, 871, 888, 949, 1115, 1142. See also, Crime, Police.

NORTH-WEST REBELLIONS, see under Military.

NOVA SCOTIA, 497, 716, 854, 937. See also under, Politics, Religious, Settlers, Social, Travel.

ONTARIO, see under Politics, Religious, Settlers, Social, Travel.

PAINTING, see Arts.

INDEX

PIONEERS, see Settlers.

POLICE, 178, 222, 552, 878, 1194, 1263. See also, Crime North-West Mounted.

POLITICS AND PUBLIC AFFAIRS:
National, 143, 146, 150, 157, 165, 176, 227, 229, 245 254, 313, 334, 339, 341, 424 426, 521, 527, 553, 573, 643 676, 689, 694, 736, 763, 846 873, 919, 920, 960, 961, 1005, 1016, 1032, 1077, 1086 1093, 1094, 1105, 1154, 1171 1217, 1226, 1233, 1234, 1260
British Columbia, 352, 742
Manitoba, 675, 901.
New Brunswick, 597, 1032, 1111, 1172.
Newfoundland, 1230.
Nova Scotia, 157, 587, 708 736, 850, 1039, 1059.
Ontario, 580, 733, 743, 835.
Quebec, 474, 674, 1194.

POLITICAL EXILES, see Military (Rebellion of 1837).

PRINCE EDWARD ISLAND, see under Religious, Settlers, Social.

QUAKERS, see under Religious.

QUEBEC, see under Politics, Religious, Settlers, Social Travel.

QUEBEC, Siege of, see under Military.

REBELLIONS, see under Military.

RELIGIOUS LIFE AND WORK:
Anglican, General, 24; Arctic, 153, 703; British Columbia, 179; Newfoundland 409; Nova Scotia, 602, 603; Ontario, 137, 248, 779, 817 909, 1060, 1119, 1122; Quebec, 285, 869, 913.
Baptists, 28, 111, 116, 159, 473, 805, 823, 988, 1145.
Free Church, 1092.
Methodists. General, 1134 Alberta, 1055, 1246; Arctic 611; British Columbia, 295, 1246; Labrador, 1258; Manitoba, 1038, 1089; Newfoundland, 711; Nova Scotia, 250 Ontario, 148, 275, 278, 440 500, 572, 629, 677, 693, 728 921, 963, 1038, 1214, 1231; Prince Edward Island, 237; Quebec, 1237; Saskatchewan, 1055, 1246, 1261.
Moravians. Labrador, 656.
Mormons. Ontario 398, 1064
Presbyterians. General, 292, 1101; British Columbia 279; New Brunswick, 171; Nova Scotia, 754, 766, 952, 1108; Ontario, 26, 131, 194 223, 433, 438, 738, 764, 861 865, 965, 995, 1022, 1047; Saskatchewan, 766.
Quakers. Ontario, 358.
Roman Catholics. General, 35, 152, 243, 263; Arctic, 173, 1045, 1137; Quebec, 319 609, 615, 670, 672, 784, 802 920, 982, 1186; New Brunswick, 948; Nova Scotia, 411 687, 948; Ontario, 367, 966 Prince Edward Island, 635.
United Church. Ontario, 1027; Saskatchewan, 1123.
Universalism, 514.
Unclassified sects. General, 1, 15, 17, 35, 186, 234 413, 444, 451, 456, 480, 497 545, 551, 770, 856, 908, 1095 1173, 1204, 1267; Alberta, 886, 1025; Arctic, 1034; British Columbia, 268, 944;

INDEX

Labrador, 85, 274, 502, 600 822; Newfoundland, 855, 1240 Nova Scotia, 93, 571, 864, 976; Ontario, 192, 197, 907 972, 1034, 1046, 1203, 1236 1259; Saskatchewan, 24, 575

RADIO, see Arts.

RAILWAYS, 155, 276, 423, 495, 534, 589, 824, 840, 936, 1118, 1171, 1235.

RANGERS, 76.

RANCHING, Alberta and Manitoba 287, 386, 400, 612, 682, 925 1168, 1274. See also Settlers

RED CROSS, 401.

ROMAN CATHOLICS, see under Religious.

SASKATCHEWAN, see under North-West Mounted, Politics, Religious, Settlers, Social, Travel.

SCIENCE (botany, geology, etc) 80, 130, 360, 481, 630, 685 705, 781, 792, 825, 840, 922 1054, 1057, 1061, 1089, 1105 1112, 1167, 1198.

SEAMEN, 112, 114, 136, 244, 269, 290, 349, 616, 624, 634 637, 651, 709, 816, 969, 1001, 1002, 1271. See also, Naval, Naval Exploration, Voyages.

SETTLERS AND FARMERS, including pioneering, clearing, social life, emigration, etc.
General, 11, 170, 219, 702 1114, 1210, 1255.
Alberta, 610, 830, 858, 874, 951, 1014, 1107, 1126.
British Columbia, 115, 121 249, 372, 408, 441, 624, 922 929, 934, 971, 985.
Labrador, 226, 319.
Manitoba, 77, 387, 406, 449, 469, 524, 564, 698, 722 727, 732, 790, 853, 983, 1256.
New Brunswick, 124, 391, 706, 1244.
Newfoundland, 731, 1244.
Ontario, 4, 23, 78, 89, 117, 135, 142, 182, 195, 231 253, 255, 256, 271, 277, 288 289, 326, 399, 407, 412, 415 428, 435, 452, 459, 468, 472 484, 492, 520, 530, 548, 550 560, 569, 576, 585, 588, 590 606, 614, 628, 639, 647, 664 666, 677, 689, 691, 694, 748 749, 812, 848, 849, 879, 881 884, 894, 900, 915, 923, 942 954, 986, 989, 996, 1008, 1010, 1042, 1051, 1052, 1065 1077, 1083, 1090, 1091, 1120 1128, 1139, 1154, 1155, 1178 1184, 1216, 1221, 1225, 1254 1273, 1274.
Prince Edward Island, 783 1051.
Quebec, 128, 322, 340, 432 468, 905, 906, 1071, 1183.
Saskatchewan, 73, 74, 75, 103, 125, 141, 224, 260, 555 619, 725, 727, 729, 748, 794 874, 935, 964, 1040, 1050, 1081, 1107, 1169, 1220, 1262

SKI-ING, see Sport.

SLAVES, 365, 566, 1015, 1117.

SOCIAL LIFE:
British Columbia, 230, 529 567, 577, 583, 742, 818, 999 1211.
New Brunswick, 95, 597, 1087, 1116, 1215.
Newfoundland, 201, 967, 977.
Nova Scotia, 937, 1072, 1087.
Ontario, 364, 494, 538, 539, 825, 831, 857, 930,

INDEX

1067, 1121, 1156.
   Prince Edward Island, 1087
   Quebec, 87, 126, 532, 559
615, 657, 663, 671, 688, 717
791, 892.

SOCIETY AND OFFICIAL SOCIAL LIFE, 2, 184, 199, 293, 370 377, 392, 489, 504, 1069, 1191. See also, Governors-General, and Politics.

SPORT:
   General, 8, 98, 99, 270, 323, 413, 519, 531, 535, 582 641, 826, 947, 1011, 1023, 1161, 1189.
   Climbing, 18, 631, 837, 911, 916, 1268.
   Fishing, 3, 363, 604, 634 854, 1098.
   Hunting, 246, 395, 428, 627, 696, 854, 926, 945, 1037, 1057, 1058, 1061, 1106 1129, 1219.

SURVEYING, 233, 439, 496, 584 650, 834, 836, 979, 993, 1079, 1247.

TAVERNS AND HOTELS, 181, 352.

TEMPERANCE MOVEMENT, 296, 311 514, 728, 806, 1015, 1257, 1258.

TRAVEL:
   General, including transcontinental and foreign, 21 61, 84, 94, 129, 167, 169, 241, 262, 266, 281, 309, 325 328, 344, 383, 384, 402, 447 455, 478, 488, 493, 533, 570 595, 620, 638, 653, 662, 679 680, 684, 704, 713, 721, 730 759, 771, 803, 813, 829, 841 859, 862, 897, 904, 914, 953 957, 974, 980, 984, 1006, 1035, 1044, 1066, 1068, 1076 1078, 1085, 1113, 1135, 1143 1144, 1149, 1188, 1193, 1269

   Arctic, 10, 104, 247, 531 582, 605, 651, 777, 928, 939 1174.
   British Columbia, 13, 110 151, 307, 369, 625, 686, 753 776, 893, 1112.
   Maritime Provinces, 12, 63 218, 324, 396, 630, 891, 912
   Labrador, 591, 592, 626.
   Ontario, 6, 66, 67, 134, 139 161, 172, 207, 265, 388, 430 477, 499, 503, 554, 586, 632 646, 665, 668, 699, 712, 743 792, 814, 852, 959, 994, 1157, 1208.
   Quebec, 65, 139, 207, 208 517, 646, 981.
   Saskatchewan, 125, 132, 145, 421, 739.

UNITED CHURCH, see under Religious.

UNIVERSALISM, see under Religious.

VOYAGES, 57, 431, 867, 993. See also, Naval, Naval Exploration, Seamen.

WAR OF 1812, see under Military.

WORLD WAR I and WORLD WAR II, see under Military.

WRITERS, NOVELISTS, POETS, 162 213, 217, 272, 301, 357, 482 505, 648, 673, 678, 700, 715 943, 1030, 1039, 1056, 1062

YUKON, see Goldrush.

ZOUAVES, 367, 1019.

www.ingramcontent.com/pod-product-compliance
Lightning Source LLC
Chambersburg PA
CBHW021712230426
43668CB00008B/815